Burl Ives'
Tales of
America

Books by Burl Ives

WAYFARING STRANGER

THE BURL IVES SONG BOOK

BURL
IVES'

IVES

TALES OF
AMERICA

WITH DECORATIONS BY HELEN BORTEN

The World Publishing Company

CLEVELAND AND NEW YORK

FIRST EDITION

Library of Congress Catalog Card Number: 54-8177

HC 954

TO

Norma and Emery Gifford II

ACKNOWLEDGEMENTS

WHEN I was very young, there was my own family, with stories of relatives who were river boatmen, sailors, and preachers. Later, at seventeen, I began to travel about the country, and everywhere there have been the old folks and their songs and stories, and the songs and stories young folks heard from their parents and grandparents. There have been the writers and the librarians and the professors and the book lovers—all of whom have had a story to exchange with me, a favorite passage to read to me, a diary or a faded newspaper to introduce me to. I cannot single out all those to whom I owe so much. I can only thank them all and trust that they will approve—or would have approved, for many of them are long gone now—what I have chosen to retell of all they told me. Also, I want to express my gratitude to my wife, Helen, for helping me make order out of the chaos of miscellany. And my thanks to Sol Stember, Jeanne Sakol, Marjorie Samuel, and Aaron Bell for research help and advice. Above all, I thank Donald Friede of The World Publishing Company, for his steady guiding hand. Oh, yes, and thanks to the two young ladies, Muriel Elnan and Gloria Spoley, who took dictation and typed long hours while others slept.

Preface

I WAS BORN in America, I grew up in America, and I went to school in America. And I'm afraid that, like many Americans, I took America for granted. It was, I felt, a fine country, a fine place to be born in and to live in. But it wasn't until I had tramped the country from one end to the other with my guitar over my shoulder that I discovered how dramatic and thrilling the true history of our country really is.

Since those early days, my search for the music of our country's past has led me almost accidentally into an endlessly unrolling panorama of stories and people, a gallery of pictures of the unique personalities and fabulous happenings which went into the making of America. The things that were seen, the way they were seen; the people who conquered the frontiers and established the settlements; the humorous people, the adventurous people; the good and the bad; the true and the false—before me there was spread a tapestry as rich and colorful as any the world has to offer. And its value is all the greater for the fact that it is solely and peculiarly American in background, circumstances, and flavor. Only here could these people have lived or been invented. Only here could these things have happened.

My mind is full of the things I have learned. And, since I am by nature a collector of all kinds of things—of songs and stories and tidbits of information, and of people who have things to tell me or who can open up new paths for me to explore—I have managed to assemble notes and jottings and clippings and books and documents, and all manner of material which overflow my bookcases and my files. From all these things I have been jotting down my own notes and writing my own stories, and doing this has given me much joy.

ix

PREFACE

I confess that in many cases my interpretations of people and stories are my own. You see, all the things I have put down here are living legends for me, and I tell them as I feel and live them. This is the way I sing my songs, too. And just as each song requires a special kind of singing so each of the tales in these pages required a special kind of telling. For this book is a variety show of legends and facts, clippings, letters, and tall tales—of the true and comic and sad things which, in the short space of three and a half centuries, made the country we know out of the rugged and dangerous shores our forefathers discovered.

—BURL IVES

May 1, 1954

Contents

CONTENTS

xii

CONTENTS

Burl Ives'
Tales of
America

FROM

A Wayfarer's Notebook:
Seventeenth Century

WE ARE SO used to the enthusiasm of local chambers of commerce in every part of the United States about the climate and health of their particular section that it is not surprising to us when we find a similar attitude expressed about the New England climate, way back in 1630, by one Reverend Francis Higginson:

> *The air of New England is one special thing that commends this place. Experience shows that there is hardly a more healthful place to be found in the world, or one that agrees better with our English bodies. Many who were weak and sickly in Old England, by coming hither, have been safely healed, and grown healthful and strong. A sup of New England's air is better than a whole draught of Old England's ale.*

❋

A TENDENCY to enforce prohibition seems to have been in the minds of some Americans from the very beginning. There is an interesting entry in Winthrop's *Journal* for the year 1639 recording the passing of an ordinance . . .

> . . . *to abolish that vain custom of drinking one to another, and that upon these and other grounds:*

3

1. *It was a thing of no good use.*
2. *It was an inducement to drunkenness, and occasion of quarreling and bloodshed.*
3. *It occasioned much waste of wine and beer.*
4. *It was very troublesome to many, especially the masters and mistresses of the feast, who were forced thereby to drink more oft than they would, etc. Yet divers (even goodly persons) were very loath to part with this idle ceremony, although (when disputation was tendered) they had no list, nor, indeed, could find any arguments, to maintain it. Such power hath custom, etc.*

One can only think in regard to the first point that obviously the early Americans had not developed the excuse of using whiskey as a medicine. As for the second point, the nature of the inducement still holds. The third point would depend upon how one defines waste, and, as for the fourth point, who would wish to leave a good party, even today?

*

THAT GOD should give mankind not only the sun for light but also light from a hitherto unknown insect, the firefly, for reading at night, seemed extremely plausible to the Englishmen who had never seen fireflies before they arrived on this continent. A chap called Thomas Ash, who had traveled in Carolina, published a book called *Carolina Beasts* in 1680, in which he had this to say about fireflies:

There are in Carolina great numbers of fireflies who carry their lanterns in their tails, in dark nights flying through the air, shining like streaks of fire and lighting it with their golden spangles. . . . [These] have two lights upon their eyes and a third in their tails; on dark nights they shine like candles so that I have often, at a distance, mistaken their sparkle for some distant plantation. With three of these fireflies secured in a glass bottle in a very dark night I have read very small print.

*

PENN, the founder of Pennsylvania, abhorred smoking. One day his Quaker council, observing him approach, laid down their pipes. "I am glad to see," said Penn, "that you are ashamed of that vile habit."

"Not at all" said a Friend, "we only lay down our pipes lest we should offend *a weak brother.*"

Love Story

A doctor once told me, after hearing me sing "Barbara Allen," that while he liked the song he refused to believe that anyone could die of love. "The human body," he said, "takes a lot of killing." I disagree with the good doctor. There are Lover's Leaps and Heartbreak Hills all over the world. I feel certain that they did not lightly come by their names. They were named, I believe, because of something that really happened. And so it is not difficult for me to believe that a beautiful Indian maiden died for the love of an English sailor.

I N THE early days of America, when Virginia was still a wilderness, a beautiful, dark-eyed Indian maiden, Arionde, lived in a settlement called Agawam. The wigwams were pitched on top of a hill which is now called Ipswich. Although Arionde had seen only a few white men, she was afraid of them, for she had heard stories of their cruelty and wickedness.

One spring morning, while strolling along the seashore, she heard a voice. It was sweet and musical and sang of happiness and good will. She turned and came face to face with a smiling youth of her own age, an English sailor left behind by his ship. Her heart beat quickly in fear. But the young sailor looked at her with soft eyes, and she did not run away.

"My name is Jeff," he said.

She did not understand his words, but his voice and smile dispelled her fears. Somehow, even without a common language, they seemed to understand each other. A look, a smile, a soft voice—these said enough. Arionde and the sailor fell in love.

9

Within a week Arionde led her lover into the Indian camp and presented him to the tribe. All made him welcome save only the maiden's former suitors. But so great was the love Arionde and Jeff bore for each other that even they became reconciled to the match.

Jeff found life among the simple Indians of Agawam agreeable and pleasant, and soon learned to talk their language. He became an expert hunter and fisherman, and the Indians, admiring and amazed, watched as his skill with the bow and arrow equaled theirs in only a few weeks.

Autumn came, then winter. And winter was not as pleasant as the summer had been. The long, cold days and nights brought with them dreams of warm English taverns, old friends and home. Jeff began to long for the sight of a sail.

One day, hunting alone along the coast some miles from Agawam, he saw a ship coming toward him. With mounting excitement, he signaled to it, and presently, a small boat came ashore.

"Englishmen!" he cried joyously.

It was a happy meeting. Speaking English for the first time in many months, Jeff answered their questions about the country and the Indians. When he learned that the ship was soon returning to England from Jamestown, he asked for passage. They agreed to take him.

Elated at the idea of once more seeing his homeland, Jeff asked them to wait the night. "I will meet you here tomorrow at dawn and go with you to Jamestown. First, I must go to Agawam."

At the Indian camp he took Arionde in his arms. "Only a short time," he said, "and I shall return to you. Wait for me," he begged, and said farewell to the weeping maiden.

Time went by, and the seasons passed. Every day the dark-eyed girl climbed the tallest hill overlooking the sea and searched the great water for a ship that would bring her lover back to her.

It was a stormy winter day when the lovely Arionde sighted

a lofty sail bearing in toward the shore. The wind from the northwest howled and shrieked, great waves piled against the rocks with the sound of thunder. The ship came nearer and nearer, obviously fighting to make harbor. She was having difficulty keeping in the channel, the furious gale and churning waters drawing her nearer and nearer to the shoal rocks and destruction.

The girl kept her station, praying to the Great Manitou to save the ship. She knew that her lover must be aboard. The breakers lashed the rocks, the wind howled. Arionde stood out on the storm-whipped cliff, buffeted by wind and rain, powerless. The unmanageable vessel was driven on the shoal, hurled onto the shore by the foaming breakers, and smashed against the rocks by the angry, roaring gray water. As its timbers went floating away on the frothing billows, a white despairing face was lifted to her for a second.

"Jeff," cried the girl. "Jeff!"

The vision sank into the heaving waves and was gone forever.

From that day, the beautiful Arionde wasted away. Her reason left her and the yellow sickness claimed her before the snow had gone from the land. She lies on the cliff, buried beside her place of watching and waiting. Today it is called Heartbreak Hill.

EPILOGUE

The townsfolk tell us that on moonlight nights there is an indescribable brightness on the tree at the top of Heartbreak Hill. Some claim to have seen two figures that thin to air as one approaches, and they say it is the two lovers reunited forever in death at the place where Arionde kept vigil.

The Story of a Princess

In the pages of the old Baldwin Reader *I first saw the picture, and then heard the story—because this was before I could read—of Pocahontas and how she saved the life of Captain John Smith. Pocahontas fascinated me. She was as real to me at that time as Alice in Wonderland, Little Miss Muffett, or Santa Claus. It was not until a few years ago when a friend showed me the diary of Captain Smith and some early John Rolfe letters that I discovered that there was a great deal more to the story of the Indian princess and John Smith than the* Baldwin Reader *had revealed to my childish eye.*

ONCE UPON a time, a long time ago when Elizabeth was queen of England, there was a king in America, whose name was Powhatan. Powhatan lived at Werowocomoco, a village on the Pamunkey River. This village was in the part of the earth which we now call Virginia. Powhatan's domain was green and fertile; there were many rivers, and many wild beasts roamed. His people hunted and fished for their food, and they also grew corn.

In the year that a princess was born to this king, there lived in England a young boy of fifteen whose name was John Smith. That very year he ran away from his home in Lincolnshire and went to sea. He was an adventurous lad, and wherever English trading vessels went—to all the ports in the exciting continent of Europe—this boy went, too. He traveled for over ten years before he returned home again, and he became strong and valiant, powerful of body and able to command. When he returned to England, he was twenty-six years old.

He heard stories about the far-off country beyond the sea, and decided that in that distant country he would find adventure and riches. He joined a group of men who called themselves the "London Company," and he helped them to get a charter from his king and gather together people who might be willing to go to this new country.

So it was that one rainy, dismal London morning in December, 1606, John Smith stood on the deck of a ship, looking back upon the shores of the country where he had been born. He was aboard the *Susan Constant*, a vessel of about one hundred tons, Captain Christopher Newport in command. With him were seventy-one men, and all kinds of supplies and weapons for establishing a colony in the wilderness. Two other ships made up the expedition. There was the barque *God Speed*, a forty-ton ship with fifty-two men crowded aboard. Her commander was Captain Bartholomew Gosnold, the famous seaman who had already been to America in 1602 and who had discovered and named Cape Cod. There was also a tiny pinnace of twenty tons; crowded as the others, she carried twenty persons aboard. Her captain was John Ratcliffe, another famous sea captain.

Much of the deck space of the *Susan Constant* was occupied by a partially built shallop (the frame of a boat that had no keel and could be used to explore shallow waters). The sailors and most of the passengers had to sleep on what little space was left on the deck. John did not mind. He found it better topside than between decks where there was no head room and one had to stoop or crawl, where there was no light and air, and where, if the hatches were battened down in a storm, the smell was unbearable. He had nothing but contempt for the groans and grumbling of his fellow passengers. They were soft, unused to traveling, "gentlemen"—as they so often reminded him.

It proved to be a long, hard voyage. Tempers frayed, per-

:onalities clashed. The greatest offender was hot-tempered young Smith, who finally argued himself into irons. He was accused of not only disliking the management of Captain Newport but of attempting to take over the ship. At least this was the claim of one man, on whose word our young hero was put in the brig.

Land was sighted in March. It was the West Indies, and the company foraged for fish and birds and turtles, and fresh water for the final leg of their voyage. Another stormy month of sailing followed; it was not until late in April that they dropped anchor in the Chickahominy River, which they named the James, and went ashore.

John Smith was under arrest at the moment of the first landing. But when the ships' captains opened the orders under which they had sailed, and which had until then been kept in a sealed box, Smith was revealed to be a member of the council that was to control the colony. A trial was held, and young Smith cleared of all charges. His enemy was ordered to pay him damages of two hundred pounds.

Smith proved annoyingly obstinate to his fellow councilmen. He insisted that his suggestion for the site of the colony be followed. He reasoned well, for he explained that the three ships could be so anchored that their guns could protect the little colony in case of an attack by the inhabitants of the country. The wisdom of this became apparent not more than a month after their arrival. With the small shallop young Smith explored and mapped what we now call the Chesapeake Bay. He was looking for the northwest passage to China. When he returned, he found that the colony, called Jamestown, had been attacked. But his foresight in choosing the site of the colony was admitted by all, enemies and friends alike, for only the ships' guns had forced the attackers to retreat.

Now let it be said immediately that neither John Smith nor the others had regard for, or understanding of, the inhabitants of this country. They thought of them as savage natives and from the very beginning considered them of no account. That is why so many of them wrote home to England that this country which they had found was "uninhabited except by aborigines."

Natives they were, but hardly to be dismissed so lightly. The great conqueror, King Powhatan, ruled many miles of this land. This king and his people were to prove very important to the inexperienced colonists.

At the time John Smith and the other colonists landed in Virginia, Powhatan was sixty years old. Well-proportioned, majestic in bearing, he was one of the greatest hunters of all the hunters of his country. Whenever there was fighting, or hardship to be endured, he still proved strongest of all. Because of this, his people loved and respected him. He had everything a king could wish for: he had conquered his enemies, his people lived well, and until the arrival of the white strangers no outsiders had threatened him. But above all, he was fortunate in that he had fathered many children. One of these, born to him by his favorite wife when he was forty-seven years old, was a female child. To this princess he gave the name Pocahontas.

The young princess was straight and tall and beautiful. She lived happily in the forest with her father, the king. Then, when she was thirteen years old, she heard much excited talk from her father and his council. She learned that strangers of a very light skin had come once again to the shores of her country. She heard that they were wicked people. They had come once before, about twenty years earlier, and had committed a barbarous act that Powhatan had not forgiven. A silver cup had disappeared from the dwelling of the white men's leader, Sir Richard Grenville, and, believing the Indians "a thieving lot," Sir Richard and his men had punished them by burning an entire Indian village to the ground. Hearing this story, young Pocahontas was very frightened and decided that she would hide if these bad men came to her village.

18

It was young John Smith's duty to trade with the Indians. On the success of this trading hung the lives of the colonists. It was difficult to conduct, partly because of language but also for other reasons. Lack of sufficient men to face the hundreds of savages living in the wilderness, lack of proper clothing, and insufficient knowledge of the forest were but a few of the obstacles. Yet it had to be done and John Smith set out to find Powhatan.

To make the task more bitter, it was winter. The colonists had no food. The English gentlemen who made up the colony were unused to working the land and had not planted during the summer. The few artisans of the group were craftsmen in gold, who had come over in the hope that this precious metal would be discovered. And there was a perfumer; he certainly served no practical purpose. In the council itself there had been nothing but wrangling. The burden of sustaining life fell on Smith.

Gathering a few men together, he set off for Werowocomoco, twelve miles away, to seek out Powhatan. He was prepared to barter trinkets, guns, and alcohol for food. But Powhatan did not condescend to see him. Instead he sent a minor chief, who listened courteously enough to Smith, and accepted the gift of a gun. In return, he put a fistful of grain in Smith's hand. Quick to recognize the insult, Smith ordered his men to fire on the assembled savages who raced into the forest and disappeared among the trees.

So hungry were Smith's soldiers that he had to restrain them from falling upon the corn heaps at once. He was sure that the Indians would reassemble and attack in great number. He was right. In the forefront of their attack, the Indians carried an idol made of skins, stuffed with moss, painted and hung with chains and copper. Greatly outnumbered, the white men escaped massacre only by a clever stratagem of Smith's. He maneuvered the capture of the idol. Seeing their talisman in enemy hands, the Indians surrendered, and Smith was able to bargain for a great store of their crops.

So it was that in one way or another Smith managed to feed his people in Jamestown. He was more fortunate in his dealings with Powhatan's other chiefs. By continuous trading he kept the colonists alive throughout the winter.

At winter's end Smith was once again forced to seek out Powhatan. Once again he marched to Werowocomoco. When he arrived, neither Powhatan nor any of his men were at home. The only member of the chief's family present was his daughter, the Princess Pocahontas.

Pocahontas and her women were at first frightened at the sight of the white men and fled to the forest. For a while they watched the white men from a safe distance. When it became obvious that the men were planning to stay in the village for the night, Pocahontas finally led her women back into the village. Smith, who by now spoke the Indian tongue, courteously addressed the young girl.

By his courtesy and the quiet discipline of his men, he won her trust. The women set food before the visitors, and then showed them to lodgings.

Smith arose at daybreak, breakfasted with the princess, and found her as lovely as he thought a savage could be. She was slender as a reed, dignified in bearing and courteous of manner. She was beautiful. The Princess Pocahontas looked on the white man with favor too. He had piercing black eyes and a full blond beard, and he was strong and a leader. The morning sun, the blue sky, and all of nature were in harmony.

But Smith, with a duty to perform, wondered when Powhatan would return. Pocahontas told him of a village farther on where he would be well received and given much corn. As they left, one of Smith's lieutenants remarked on the feast and their treatment, "Call ye them savages? If these be savages in the whole conception, where then shall we look for a civilized man?"

Smith turned to his companion, "Have you no eyes? In the right side of that tent was strung seven and twenty fresh scalps. It is luck they were not English."

It was not long afterward that Smith and nine companions went on a foraging trip up the Chickahominy River. At Apocant he took two men ashore, and ordered the others to stay aboard the boat and protect it. Unfortunately, the men left on the boat grew restive and went ashore. One of them was captured by Opecanchanough, Powhatan's brother, and tortured into telling where John Smith could be found. Smith and his two companions, twenty miles inland, were unaware there were Indians around them until they, too, were attacked. The two men with Smith were killed, and he would have been also had he not grabbed an Indian in hand-to-hand combat and held him as a shield. He retreated fighting, with the squirming Indian as protection.

A ridiculous mishap caused Smith's capture. He fell backward into a muddy creek and was unable to extricate himself. The Indian, falling on top of him, saved his life; the barrage of arrows intended for Smith killed the Indian instead.

Smith was dragged from the mire expecting at any moment to die. Instead he was brought before a fire, trembling with cold and wet. His captors warmed him, and their women rubbed his limbs. After which Opecanchanough led him from village to village, exhibiting him to the Indians. It was almost a month later that Smith was brought to Werowocomoco.

Smith was taken to Powhatan's headquarters. There he was brought into the council wigwam, where Powhatan sat on a dais, young women on either side of him. His warriors sat in rows along the sides of the wigwam and behind them stood their women. The heads and shoulders of the warriors were painted red, and Smith estimated there were two hundred of them present. Water was brought for Smith's hands and a bunch of feathers given him as a towel. He was then feasted; all the while a long consultation was held among the Indians. When they concluded their discussion two stones were dragged in, Smith's hands were retied, and he was forced to lay his head upon the stones. The seated Indians arose and held their war clubs in readiness.

Suddenly there was an interruption. The young girl, Pocahontas, knelt beside Smith and begged his life of her father. Powhatan pulled the girl to her feet and reasoned with her. She would not be solaced. Finally Powhatan set aside the death sentence and decreed that Smith be made to work as a slave.

Smith was taken to the wigwam of Powhatan. There, in her father's lodge, Pocahontas busied herself with household duties. Not once did she acknowledge Smith's thanks or return his glances. More receptive to Smith's advances was Nantaquaus, Powhatan's oldest son. The two young men would sit together and talk of their differences and their countries. It was Nantaquaus who told Smith that the tribe planned to make him an artisan, sewing robes and shoes, making bows and arrows for Powhatan.

How this was to be, Smith could not determine since he was notoriously clumsy with his hands. He explained this to Nantaquaus. The young brave appealed to Powhatan: certainly this great fighter and hunter should not be a slave, Nantaquaus argued. And his arguments prevailed. It was decided to adopt Smith into the tribe.

He was taken to a great ceremonial lodge in the woods and left alone before a lighted fire. The room was dark beyond the firelight. He sat tensely, wondering what would be expected of him. Suddenly he jumped with fright. A most doleful and frightening noise seemed to be coming from all sides. Fearful as he was, he sat stoically as though hearing nothing, for he knew he was being watched. All at once into the fire's light leaped two hundred painted savages. But no matter what they did, Smith sat unmoving, and so it was he became a member of the tribe and was adopted by Powhatan as his son.

As one of the Powhatans, Smith was given food for his people and allowed to return to Jamestown. Pocahontas became a constant visitor at his home there . . . this, it is firmly believed, without the knowledge of her father. She became friendly with the people of the colonies; she went aboard their ships and into their houses. English became familiar to her, and soon she could converse with those around her at Jamestown.

Now Smith's bargaining power depended not only upon his membership in Powhatan's tribe but also upon the value the chief put upon English-made objects. In the spring Captain Newport returned to Jamestown with authority to take over the complete administration of the colony. Captain Newport gave freely of too many gifts. Smith was infuriated but powerless. It was only for the good of the colony that he agreed to accompany Newport as an interpreter when the latter decided to take over trading with Powhatan.

At Powhatan's wigwam, Newport began bargaining with him. Finally the chief arose: "Captain Newport," he said, "it is not agreeable to my greatness in this piddling manner to trade for trifles; and I esteem you also a great warrior. Therefore, lay me down all your commodities together; what I like I will take and in recompense give you what I think fitting their value."

Newport turned over his goods and was given in return three bushels of corn instead of the twenty hogsheads he had expected. In the presence of the Indians, he turned and spoke angrily to Smith. Conscious of his dignity before Indian eyes, Smith did not answer. He merely turned from the irate Newport and, as if by chance, took from his own pocket a long string of beautiful blue beads.

Pocahontas immediately pleaded with her father to buy the beads. Smith refused to sell, saying they were his only by accident, were of a great price, and could be worn only by great kings. No matter how high Powhatan's offers went, Smith put the beads away and refused to sell. He was finally brought around by the begging of Pocahontas. At her importuning, and with a great show of reluctance, Smith finally handed over the beads. He accepted in return three hundred bushels of corn.

Newport left the country after this, in the summer of 1608. Smith once again negotiated with Powhatan. According to his diary, their relationship was a fluctuating one. Still, Smith almost always got his way, for the two men respected and understood each other. At one time Powhatan made a speech to Smith in which he said: "I am not so simple as not to know it is better to eat good meat, lie well, and sleep quietly with my women and children; to laugh and be merry with the English, and be their friend, to have copper, hatchets and whatever else I want, than to fly from all to lie cold in the woods, feeding upon acorns, roots and such, and to be so hunted that I cannot rest, eat or sleep. In such circumstances, my men must watch, and if a twig should be brake, all would cry out, 'Here comes Captain Smith'; and so in this miserable manner to end my miserable life; and, Captain Smith, this might be soon your fate, too, through your rashness. I therefore exhort you to peaceable councils and above all I insist that you come not with guns and swords, the cause of all our jealousies and uneasiness."

Shortly after this, Smith went on an exploring expedition toward the falls of the James River. He carried his powder in bags at his belt. The first night out, he and his men lighted a fire to cook dinner. Smith stood looking up at the towering trees; he listened to the fall of the water and could not help but wonder when he would return to England again. A burning ember shot from the fire and, without his noticing it, fell on the surface of one of the powder bags he wore. There was a sudden burst of light as first one bag and then the other exploded. By the time Smith's men extinguished the blaze, he was very badly burned on his body and his face.

Pain-racked and feverish, Smith was carried through the forest on a litter to Jamestown, and after a while it was decided that he should return to England. He sailed on October 4, 1609, and never set foot in Virginia again.

Princess Pocahontas came to Jamestown and found that

Smith was gone. If a message had been left, she did not receive it. She went sadly back to her father's wigwam and did not return to Jamestown for four years.

Pocahontas lived quietly with her people. That she was bitter seemed evident for she refused again and again to see English people.

One day she relented. With a minor Powhatan chief and his squaw, she boarded an English ship anchored in the Potomac River. Leaving her companions, Pocahontas sought out the gun room where she and Smith had once sat. She was followed by the Master of the ship, Captain Argall, and told that she was a prisoner, a hostage for her father's good behavior.

For two years, Pocahontas was a captive of the English. So courteously and kindly was she treated, however, that she adjusted to English customs. She dressed in English clothes and became a part of the Argall family life.

A young man of Jamestown, who had admired Pocahontas when she used to visit the settlement, became a constant visitor on board the ship where she was held prisoner. It was not the custom of the English at this time to intermarry with the natives of the country. There were stories of Frenchmen to the north and of Spaniards to the south taking native women as wives, but the Jamestown colonists had thus far refrained from such intermarriage. John Rolfe resisted the attractions of Pocahontas as long as he could. But love proved too strong at last, and he wrote to his parents in London that he was in love, and with one ". . . whose education hath bin rude, her manners barbarous, her generation accursed."

After two years it seemed that their attachment was mutual. The British governor, Sir Thomas Dale, and his wife, did much to educate and improve Pocahontas in English manners. She was a willing student for, as she said, this was the way of life in England, where Captain John Smith lived.

Rolfe finally decided that he must marry Pocahontas. She

refused his first offer on the grounds that her father and brothers would not approve. Rolfe, however, was a man of decision, and at his insistence Sir Thomas Dale took the ship on which Pocahontas was confined up the river to Powhatan's residence. After a series of skirmishes and misunderstandings, Pocahontas's brothers came aboard the ship and greeted their sister for the first time in two years. After a tearful reunion, Pocahontas sent a message to old Powhatan. Most of all, she wanted to know how her father would feel about her proposed marriage to an Englishman.

Receiving Powhatan's blessing, she agreed to the marriage, and the wedding took place on April 16, 1614. On her wedding day, Pocahontas became a member of the English church and was baptized Rebecca. From that time on, Powhatan treated all Englishmen with great cordiality.

By 1614, many Indians had gone willingly, or unwillingly, to visit the English court. None, however, had had such a romantic history nor were so well received as the beautiful Princess Pocahontas. When she was presented at court, so charming were her manners and so delicate her speech that she was an immediate favorite.

Rolfe's bringing of his bride to England was responsible for a last strange chapter in the story of Captain John Smith and the Indian princess.

After her long voyage, Pocahontas felt cheated when she learned that Captain Smith had gone on an expedition to New England. As she explained to her husband, she had looked forward to seeing him again since he had once been her best friend in America.

But at last Smith returned to London. Pocahontas tried to see him at once, but Smith kept putting off their meeting. Then Pocahontas learned that Smith was to be at court on a certain day and immediately decided that she would be there also.

Captain Smith was already in the antechamber to the bedroom of King James I when the beautiful bronze-complexioned princess from America entered. It was court gossip that she was anxious to meet her old friend; lords and ladies in waiting watched curiously as she glided across the room to confront him.

She stood before him waiting for him to speak. He greeted her coldly and said that she looked well. Offended by his coldness, she exclaimed, "Father! Do you not know me? Why do you speak so to me?"

The captain, much embarrassed, glanced nervously at the listening ladies and gentlemen and said as coldly as before, "Do not call me father." (He explained later that he spoke thus because he felt it would give offense to royalty for him to be called the father of a king's daughter.)

A flush of anger colored the Lady Rebecca's cheek, and she was silent for some time. Then she said to Smith in a low voice, "You were not afraid to come into my father's country and strike fear into everybody but myself; and are you here afraid to let me call you father? I tell you I will call you father, and you shall call me child; and so I will forever be of your kindred and country."

When Smith still did not respond, Pocahontas said, "They always told us that you were dead, and I knew not otherwise until I came to your country." Smith raised his eyes and for a long moment these two looked at each other. Then the Lady Rebecca turned away.

EPILOGUE

They told the Lady Rebecca that whenever Captain Smith spoke of her it was always with respect. She saw him seldom after this meeting, and then only at a distance.

Pocahontas was twenty-two years old when she was suddenly overwhelmed by a great desire to go back to her own country and her own people, if only for a little while. Before

*she could leave London, she discovered she was pregnant and
waited there for the birth of her son, Thomas Rolfe. She
planned to take the child to America with her for the visit, but
she fell sick and died before boarding ship.*

The Ghost and Hans Van Duin

I have felt the presence of ghosts several times in my life. I saw one last year. There are very few left in the cities, I'm told, what with so much noise and the constant tearing down and building up. A ghost cannot abide it all. But in the countryside, in the old and creaking houses . . .

MANY years before the English took New Amsterdam from the Dutch and renamed it New York, there lived in that village—for it wasn't more than a village then—a happy-go-lucky young scamp named Hans Van Duin. Always getting into mischief, playing pranks, and in general giving people something to talk about besides the weather and the fear of Indian raids, he was well liked. Besides he was very liberal in treating anyone he met in the ale houses. Here it was that he freely spent the money of his old father, Hendrick Van Duin.

There was only one thing in life that Hans disliked and that was work. Of this he did as little as possible. To those who spoke to Hans seriously about his shiftless ways, he would merely say, "Why should I work? My grandfather left me a great deal of money."

Now this was only true in theory, for while Hans's grandfather had been a very wealthy man, no one had ever been able to find his money after he died. As a matter of fact, the grandfather's son, old Hendrick, as a young man had had to go quietly about opening a business of his own, a ships' chandlery. He did well enough at this to give Hans the means to play like the proverbial grasshopper.

One cold night old Hendrick passed away. He left Hans a little money, but not very much, and Hans soon spent it. Those he had bought for at the taverns did not return the

31

favor when Hans was thirsty, so eventually he was forced to look for work. Many there were who would not have anything to do with such a wastrel, but a doctor of the town took him into service. He did his work well, but not with as merry a disposition or as prankish a nature as before.

Now Hans had not been with the doctor more than a few months when his employer was offered the bargain of a farm located some distance outside of town. It was quite far out . . . being at what is now 23rd Street. What the doctor did not know was that the owner was selling because he could not keep tenants to work the farm. Without exception all who tried to live there complained of ghosts and strange noises. Not only were there no profits but indeed sometimes the owner had not even made enough for expenses. When the doctor first heard of this it was too late; the farm was already his.

Unlike most of the people of the time, Hans declared that he did not believe in the supernatural. (This was one of the many ways in which Hans differed from the others.) So the doctor decided that Hans should tend to the running of the farm for a year and sent him there to live on it alone.

Filled with the spirit of adventure, thinking that not only would he perhaps make a fortune in farming but that he would also have a fine time telling his tavern friends of the strange happenings at the farmhouse, Hans set out.

Hans found the farmhouse large, built of logs and stones, and well appointed. He learned from the tenant farmer who was moving out that it had been built by an old Hollander, who had lived there—unmolested by the usually hostile Indians—with a French housekeeper and two farm hands. When the old man died, leaving no relatives, the Frenchwoman and the two men had returned to Europe, and the house had been taken over by strangers.

Hans decided that, since he was the farm's master now, he would sleep in the master bedroom on the second floor. He went to bed early that evening and slept soundly, even though he had a very strange dream. He dreamt that he woke up and saw a man sitting in a chair by his bed. However, this dream did not disturb Hans, and he arose refreshed and busied himself on the land all that day. He was determined to make a success of his new venture, for he sorely missed his tavern days.

The next night, he had been asleep for a few hours when he was awakened by the solemn tread of heavy steps. At that moment the downstairs clock struck twelve. For some unknown reason Hans had carefully bolted his bedroom door. You can imagine his terror when the footsteps stopped outside his chamber, and the bolted door softly opened.

A heavy-set old man entered the room and walked slowly toward the chair by Hans's bed. He sat down, breathed deeply, and fastened his gaze on the apparently sleeping young man. Hans lay rigid with fear. He pretended to be asleep, but he never took his barely opened eyes from the figure in the chair. In this way they watched each other all night long. When the first cock crowed, the old man heaved a deep sigh, as if in disappointment, then rose and left as he had come in. Hans waited until it was completely light, and then, mustering all his courage, went to the door. He found it bolted from the inside—just as he had left it the night before.

That day, Hans went about his business in a low, distracted state. He went to bed that night with his nerves tingling, taking with him a Bible and Book of Catechism, which he clutched to his breast for protection. He could not sleep for a single moment. When the clock struck twelve, Hans stiffened in fear, for once again he heard the footsteps approach and stop outside the bolted door. Once again the door swung open. Unable to close his eyes, Hans saw his visitor clearly this time. The old man had curly gray hair and big black eyes. He wore leather boots, a slouch hat with a wide brim, and doublet and hose. Once again the figure walked to the chair and sat down and looked fixedly at Hans. All night long they stared into

33

each other's eyes. As before, neither spoke, and at dawn the old man rose, heaved a heavy sigh, and left.

The experience filled Hans with such terror that, without a word to his employer or anyone else, he left the farm, determined never to return.

He boarded a schooner which took him up the Hudson, and disembarking at Albany, he walked along the shore of the river, wondering what he could do to earn a living in this new place.

Suddenly he heard a cry for help. Running toward the cry, Hans saw a young lady being chased by an enraged bull. Quickly he diverted the angry beast's attention, and the young lady was able to climb a fence to safety.

The young lady's father came running to the scene just as Hans himself had joined her on the safe side of the fence. There were introductions, and in gratitude, the father, a Mr. Vandenburg, invited Hans to supper.

Mr. Vandenburg of Albany was a wealthy landowner, a famous hunter, and a respected citizen. In the next few days he discovered that Hans could shoot, row, fish, and swim with skill. Mr. Vandenburg took a tremendous liking to the young man, and, since it was obvious that his lovely daughter, Gretel, felt as he did, he asked his visitor to stay on. Nothing could have suited Hans better, for not only was Mr. Vandenburg's house well appointed, but his liquor was good and his food of the finest. Hans was having a very lovely time indeed.

It took only a short time for Mr. Vandenburg to decide that Hans would make a fine son-in-law, and he began to plot. This was quite unnecessary, had he but known it; love is its own master and will seldom tolerate assistance or hindrance. And Gretel and Hans had long ago come to an understanding. But when Mr. Vandenburg suggested to Hans that he should move from the inn to the Vandenburg manor, they were both careful to conceal their pleasure from him.

Now there was one room in the Vandenburg house that

Hans had not seen. This was the guest bedroom. He was shown to this room by Gretel and her father. As they entered, Hans stopped abruptly, his eyes glued to a large painting hanging on the opposite wall.

"Why are you trembling? What's wrong?" the girl asked anxiously.

"Is something the matter?" Mr. Vandenburg inquired in surprise.

"*Whose* picture is that?" cried Hans, pointing with trembling hand at the portrait above the mantelpiece.

"An old nobleman from Holland whom my father knew," said Mr. Vandenburg. "He came to America many years ago. They say he was a miser and buried all his gold—half of which was rightly his brother's."

"What was his name?" asked Hans.

"His name was Van Duin," Mr. Vandenburg replied.

"Why," said the lovely Gretel, "it's the same as yours, Hans."

As you must have guessed by now, the picture which Hans saw was an exact likeness of the man who had come to sit beside his bed at the farm in New Amsterdam. Could the ghost be his grandfather's brother? It was with hasty explanations and the promise of a quick return that Hans said goodbye to his host the next day and caught the first boat for New Amsterdam.

Greeting no one on his arrival, Hans went immediately to the farm. He could barely wait for night to fall. When it was dark he went to bed and lay in tense expectation, still clutching the Bible and Catechism, in case he was in error.

Sure enough, as the clock struck twelve, the door opened and in came the heavy-set gentleman. As before, the ghost sat down and sighed heavily. As before, he fixed his melancholy eyes on the recumbent Hans.

"Why do you come here?" Hans asked.

When Hans spoke, what might have been a smile appeared

35

on the old ghost's face, and the eyes that before were black and forbidding seemed to twinkle. The old man did not answer, but he rose and beckoned with a gnarled finger for Hans to follow him. Crossing himself first, Hans got out of bed.

The old man went through the door without unbolting it—leaving that bit of bother to the frightened but courageous youth. He led Hans into the garden through a thicket and stopped near one of the old trees. Here he pointed twice to the ground and then vanished. On investigation, Hans found an old, unused well. Disturbing nothing, he went back to bed and slept a sweet, sound sleep.

As soon as it was day, Hans uncovered the well and began to fish in it with iron hooks. Few fishermen ever did so well. Almost at once his hook fastened onto something at the bottom of the well. Hans pulled with all his strength and up it came. Cleaning the mud from the object, he discovered that it was a silver porringer with the lid bolted down by wire. Eagerly he cut the wires and pried open the lid—it was filled to the brim with gold coins!

The well yielded more besides: receptacles filled with jewels of every description, pieces of silver engraved with the authentic coat of arms of the Van Duin family, and gold and more gold. Bit by bit, Hans carried his new-found wealth to the farmhouse and rehid it.

Later that day there was great excitement when Hans appeared in the tavern of the town. Because of his strange disappearance, the townspeople had assumed that ghosts had spirited him away. Hans encouraged them in this belief. His tales of horror kept everyone from going near the farm and gave him the opportunity to buy it.

It isn't necessary to tell you that soon Hans became a generous treater again, and all his old friends swarmed around him once more. Of course, that he had money made it obvious to many in the town that he had sold his soul to the Devil. Yet, when they saw the silver with his coat of arms, they admitted him as a substantial member of society. And when he gave a silver candelabra to the church and it did not explode or cause any harm whatsoever, the congregation as a whole finally accepted him.

Hans lived on in New Amsterdam, the jolliest, richest, most pleasant citizen on the island. He went to Albany and brought back his bride and on his return gave the greatest feast ever held in the New World. As a matter of fact, as his life progressed, he was always treating all comers at the inn to food and drink, and it was at one of his own sumptuous parties that he died . . . of apoplexy . . . standing in the middle of the inn floor, toasting the loveliest girl in the world, "his Gretel." He was celebrating his ninety-fourth birthday.

The Unwilling Pirate

Pirates have always fascinated me. Cruising the Florida Keys, or in the Bahamas, I sit in silence on the deck of my little ship and dream of the days of the free-booters. Someday, perhaps, I may discover a lead cask, full of jewels and gold pieces. Many times in my imagination has this happened to me. The stuff is there, of that there is little doubt. But it has been told me by experts in this field that all of the modern devices for recognizing metals are not as good as the man who is psychic and is led to the treasure by an instinct not unlike that of the carrier pigeon who can find his way home by circling in the air and then pointing unerringly in the right direction. I have a feeling that I shall get tuned in properly sometime. But when I do, it will not be Captain Kidd's loot that I recover. You see, there wasn't any. And, the the notorious Captain Kidd wasn't even a pirate.

FROM 1689 on, France and England waged war in America. As the war went on, England had to concentrate her fleet at home against the fleet of Louis XIV and piratical acts became increasingly frequent—and successful. Yankee merchants exchanged guns, rum, and ammunition for jewels, gold, and other merchandise, no questions asked. Cargoes could be sold most easily in New York where the port officials were bribed. Some of the most reputable men in the community were a part of this trade, and it became a code of the time that it was a sin for a pirate to divulge his political and financial backer's identity.

The name of one pirate of this period brings immediately to mind the thought of Blood and Buried Treasure: Captain

41

Kidd. Actually Captain Kidd was not a pirate at all but an exceptionally unsuccessful privateer. His story is this:

The activities of pirates and smugglers resulted in such a loss of revenue by 1696 that the English king was moved to action. Because the navy already had its hands full, a private company was formed to hunt down and destroy pirates—and also to return a profit. Stockholders in this company were King William, Lord Bellomont (then governor of New York, Massachusetts, and New Hampshire), Lord Chancellor Somers, and other noted figures. This company bought and fitted out a thirty-gun ship, the *Adventure Galley*. On Governor Bellomont's recommendation a New York merchant captain, William Kidd, was put in command with a commission and letters of marque, and orders to sail against the pirates in the Eastern seas, off Madagascar.

This was the beginning of poor Captain Kidd's troubles. He was unsuccessful in Madagascar, since the pirates had heard of his mission and fled. His crew finally grew mutinous, and demanded action. It should be explained that ships flying the colors of France or India or of piracy were considered fair prizes and to attack them was not piracy. Captain Kidd finally agreed to attack ships of this sort. The *Adventure Galley* was having great success in these activities when Kidd made the fatal mistake. He somehow became involved in a battle with an ENGLISH ship, an East Indiaman called the *Quedah Merchant*. He put her crew ashore, boarded her, and burnt his own ship.

Much notoriety resulted, notoriety that was politically inconvenient to King William and Governor Bellomont (especially since there was a temporary truce between France and England). Kidd had hit a mutinous member of his own crew, William Moore, on the head with a wooden bucket, resulting in Moore's death. On this excuse he was arrested, brought to London, and there convicted. He was sent to the gallows on the twenty-third of May, 1701.

Interestingly enough, popular sentiment was directed against him by a ballad purporting to tell his story. As a contemporary put it, Captain Kidd was hanged "by a doggerel ballad sung to a villainous tune."

Oh, my name was William Kidd, as I sailed, as I sailed,
My name was William Kidd, as I sailed,
My name was William Kidd, God's laws I did forbid,
And most wickedly I did, as I sailed, as I sailed.
And most wickedly I did as I sailed.

Oh, my parents taught me well, as I sailed, as I sailed,
My parents taught me well, as I sailed,
My parents taught me well, to shun the gates of hell,
But against them I rebelled, as I sailed, as I sailed.
But against them I rebelled as I sailed.

Oh, I murdered William Moore, as I sailed, as I sailed,
I murdered William Moore, as I sailed,
I murdered William Moore, and I left him in his gore,
Not many leagues from shore, as I sailed, as I sailed.
Not many leagues from shore as I sailed.

Oh, I steered from sound to sound, as I sailed, as I sailed,
Oh, I steered from sound to sound, as I sailed.
I steered from sound to sound, and many ships I found,
And all of them I burned, as I sailed, as I sailed,
And all of them I burned as I sailed.

And being cruel still, as I sailed, as I sailed,
And being cruel still as I sailed,
And being cruel still, my gunner I did kill,
And his precious blood did spill, as I sailed, as I sailed,
And his precious blood did spill as I sailed.

I was sick and nigh to death, as I sailed, as I sailed,
I was sick and nigh to death as I sailed.
I was sick and nigh to death and I vowed with every breath,
To walk in wisdom's ways, when I sailed, when I sailed,
To walk in wisdom's ways when I sailed.

My repentance lasted not, as I sailed, as I sailed,
My repentance lasted not, as I sailed.
My repentance lasted not, my vows I soon forgot,
Damnation was my lot, as I sailed, as I sailed,
Damnation was my lot as I sailed.

43

To the execution dock I must go, I must go,
To the execution dock I must go.
To the execution dock, while many thousands flock,
But I must bear the shock and must die, and must die,
But I must bear the shock and must die.

Take a warning now by me, for I must die, for I must die,
Take a warning now by me for I must die.
Take a warning now by me and shun bad company,
Lest you come to hell with me, for I must die, I must die,
Lest you come to hell with me, for I must die.

A Wayfarer's Notebook:
Eighteenth Century

THE PERSONAL columns of colonial newspapers carried items of all kinds. One section was called "wants." We find the following "wants" listed in a New Jersey newspaper of the 1700:

Stolen from Thomas Steeples, of Springfield, New Jersey, on the first day of March, a white horse, of low stature, well built for strength, and short backed. He has a small head, little ears, two white eyes, one whiter than the other, a long mane on the off side, curled and trimmed on the other; also a large switch tail and four white hoofs.

Any person bringing to me the horse and rider shall have five pounds reward, or for the horse alone, forty shillings reward.

John, the son of Peter Hodgkinson, a boy about 13 years of age, was taken by a Spanish privateer, in his passage from Dublin to Philadelphia on board a brigantine. His father can obtain no satisfactory account of him at present. If any person will take care of this boy if he is on the continent among English inhabitants, and send word to his father, in Burlington, New Jersey, or conduct him there, he shall receive five pounds for the said boy or reasonable satisfaction for any information.

❋

A QUAKER gentleman, riding in a carriage with a fashionable lady decked with a profusion of jewelry, heard her complaining of the cold. Shivering in her lace bonnet and shawl, as light as a cobweb, she exclaimed:

"What shall I do to get warm?"

"I really don't know," replied the Quaker solemnly, "unless thee puts on another breastpin."

❋

IT WAS an ancient conceit that if one addressed Echo, one could get back a true answer to the future. Perhaps it was because of this that echo verses became popular in the seventeenth and eighteenth centuries. In an echo verse, the last few syllables of a line are repeated in such wise that it seems to be an answer to the question asked in the line. Here is an Echo questionnaire, and answer, from a newspaper of Revolutionary times:

> What must be done to conduct a newspaper right?—Write.
> What is necessary for a farmer to assist him?—System.
> What would give a blind man the greatest delight?—Light.
> What is the best counsel given by a justice of the peace?
> —Peace.
> Who commit the greatest abominations?—Nations.
> What cry is the greatest terrifier?—Fire.
> What are some women's chief exercise?—Sighs.

❋

THE SETTLERS quickly became used to and acquired a colonial pride in the wild life and flora which were peculiarly American. The wild turkey, the corn, the rattlesnake, the sunflower, were all particular to the American continent. There is an

amusing report made by a Hessian officer who was stationed
with the British at Philadelphia. He wrote to his wife in Göt-
tingen an extremely exaggerated report on the rattlesnake.
It is possible that some of our early Philadelphians were telling this Hessian officer a tall tale—or do you suppose the
Pennsylvania rattlesnakes were particularly virulent at this
time?

> ... *Nothing, however, can be more terrible than the
> rattlesnake. Its length is from 12 to 16 feet; and its
> glance, the people living here believe, is capable of
> killing a person. Several years ago a farmer living in
> my neighborhood lost a relative in this manner. He
> had been hunting, and seeing a bear standing mo-
> tionless before him, he took aim and laid him low.
> But scarcely had he reached the bear when he him-
> self seemed transfixed, and then fell over dead. All
> this was caused by a rattlesnake that lay coiled up
> in a high tree.*

✲

ONE of President Washington's officers presented an Indian
sachem with a medal which had been struck off in Philadelphia. On one side of the medal Washington was represented,
armed with a sword; on the other side was the likeness of
an Indian in the act of burying a hatchet. The sachem refused to accept the medal, asking, "Why does not the President bury his sword, too?"

✲

ONE of the stories we most often hear about Benjamin
Franklin was that when he was formally presented at the

court of King Louis XVI of France he wore an ordinary plain suit. He was much lauded for his simplicity and his democratic courage in so dressing.

Nathaniel Hawthorne in his notebooks relates an anecdote told him by an aged lady in England, for whose veracity he vouches. She told him that the true reason for Franklin's wearing his plain suit—and this with great embarrassment—was that his tailor had disappointed him of his gold-embroidered court costume. Franklin, she said, having made a successful impression by his mistake, continued to wear plain dress everywhere as a matter of policy.

❋

FOLLOWING the death of his wife, Thomas Jefferson was much concerned about the upbringing of his daughter, Martha, whom he privately called Patsy. He wrote to her frequently and in one of his letters took up the matter of her education. He certainly believed in a busy day for the young lady when he wrote:

> *With respect to the distribution of your time, my dear Patsy, the following is what I should approve:*
> *From 8 to 10, practice music;*
> *" 10 to 1:00, dance one day and draw another;*
> *" 1:00 to 2:00, draw on the day you dance, and write a letter next day;*
> *" 3:00 to 4:00, read French;*
> *" 4:00 to 5:00, exercise yourself in music;*
> *" 5:00 till bedtime, read English, write, etc.*
> *... I expect you to write me by every post. Inform me of the books you read, what you learn and enclose me your best copy of every lesson and drawing.... Take care that you never spell a word wrong.*

48

Always before you write a word consider how it is spelt and if you do not remember it, turn to a dictionary. It produces great praise to a lady to spell well. I have placed my happiness in seeing you good and accomplished; and no distress this world can bring on me would equal that of you disappointing my hopes.

He added this postscript:

Keep my letters and read them at times, that you may always have present in your mind those things which will endear you to me.

*

AMERICAN newspaper writers commenting on the doings of their day and the people of their time have been present from colonial times to now. One, Robert Slender, published a little book in 1799 called *Letters on Various Interesting and Important Subjects.* Here is a sample of his approach and attitude:

MR. EDITOR,
Having heard that there was a tavern at about the distance of a mile or so from my favorite country spot, where now and then a few neighbors meet to spit, smoke segars, drink apple whiskey, cider or cider-royal, and read the news — a few evenings ago, I put on my best coat, combed out my wig, put my spectacles in my pocket, and a quarter dollar — This I thought was right; for although Mrs. Slender told me eleven-pence was enough, says I, I'll e'en take the quarter dollar, for a man always feels himself more of consequence when he has got good money in his pocket — so out I walks with a good stout stick in my hand, which I always make a point to

carry with me, lest the dogs should make rather freer with my legs than I could wish. But I had not gone more than half the way, when, by making a false step, I splash'd my stocking from the knee to the ancle. Odds to my heart, said I, I'll hear of this in both sides of my head — but it can't now be helped — this and a thousand worse accidents, which daily happen, are all occasioned by public neglect, and the misapplication of the public's money — Had I, said I, (talking to myself all the while) the disposal of but half the income of the United States, I could at least so order matters, that a man might walk to his next neighbor's without splashing his stockings or being in danger of breaking his legs in ruts, holes, gutts, and gullies. I do not know, says I to myself, as I moralized on my splash'd stocking, but money might with more profit be laid out in repairing the roads, than in marine establishments, supporting a standing army, useless embassies, exorbitant salaries, given to many flashy fellows that are no honor to us, or to themselves, and chartering whole ships to carry a single man to another nation — Odds my life, continued I, what a number of difficulties a man labors under, who has never read further than Lilly's grammar, and has but a poor brain — had I been favored with a good education, I could no doubt readily see the great usefulness of all these measures of government, that now appear to me so unaccountable — I could then, said I, still talking to myself, see the reason why the old patriots, whose blood flowed so freely in purchasing their independence, are cast aside, like a broken pitcher, (as the scripture says) and why the old tories and active refugees are advanced to places of power, honor and trust.

Jacob Heard and the
Golden Horse

The world of childhood is a beautiful world. The world of childhood is a world where dreams and reality move without boundary between them. Here is a story of an adult who believed in witches, and yet denied the innocent dream creations of a child.

JACOB HEARD was tall and thin. His lips were thin too and he seldom smiled. He was a good man and on excellent conversational terms with God Himself. This was because he was not only a religious Puritan, but more religious than most of the Puritans around him. His neighbors were wary of him because he worried overmuch about what they were doing. He seldom missed a church service and he never missed the hanging or burning of a witch.

Jacob was one of the people who had seen the silver bullet in Old Meg's body. He could tell you about Old Meg and about witches.

"You never know where or who they are," Jacob often said sagely about witches. "We can only see their evil work. Take Old Meg of Gloucester! That old devil had been turning milk sour, putting curses on the children to cripple them, making the cattle die, dogs go mad, and what-all. Could we be sure? . . . No, she wouldn't confess it. We got her though." And then Jacob would tell, if you asked him, the true story of Old Meg, the witch.

Old Meg, whose name was Margaret Wesson, came to her death in her own home in Gloucester by two shots *fired five hundred miles away* at the siege of Louisburg. At this battle, two soldiers who had enlisted from Gloucester were continuously annoyed by a large, skinny, black crow. This crow would fly down again and again, cawing harshly. The two soldiers

53

who were on guard duty threw stones at it, dirt clods, and pieces of wood. It finally became such a nuisance that they shot at it and were quite sure they had hit it many times. The crow returned more angry and wicked than before. The two soldiers decided that it must be a witch and believed it could be none other than Old Meg who had followed them from Gloucester. It was later discovered they had good cause for thinking so, for they had taken a pitcher of milk from her without payment.

"Only silver bullets will kill a witch," said one to the other. "I'll make a silver bullet from the button on my coat."

"And I shall make one from mine," replied his comrade.

The crow annoyed them mightily while they made the bullets of silver. Then powder was poured into the muskets and a silver bullet rammed into each. On the first shot, a leg was broken and the feathers flew. "Got her!" the first soldier cried. But he was wrong, and the screeching crow still circled over their heads. The second shot dropped the crow. The soldiers declared they would have gone near the body, but they did not because they heard Old Meg's voice cursing them as the crow breathed its last breath.

Weeks later when the soldiers returned home to Gloucester, they told their story. How surprised everyone was when it was determined that at exactly the hour and day the boys had fired the silver bullets, Old Meg had fallen and broken her leg and died an instant later.

A committee of citizens and responsible church members from other cities came to dig up Old Meg's body. They extracted silver-button bullets from her flesh.

Jacob would tell this story as first-hand evidence to those people who underestimated the importance of finding out witches.

One Sunday afternoon, Jacob Heard and his wife were sitting under the great oak tree in front of their house reading the Bible. Their son Paul was down in the meadow.

Paul Heard was beloved of his mother, but his father did not approve of the boy and often had to chastise him, for he had not the sternness or seriousness that Jacob would have wished. Sometimes Paul would walk alone and speak to himself. Jacob did not like this because the boy admitted he had not been talking with God. Also, he dreamed a lot. Jacob had to say to his wife, "It is certain he will never be a farmer or a tradesman. I shall make him a minister of the Gospel." Mrs. Heard did not answer, but she had her doubts. Paul dreamed indeed, but about flowers and birds. Only she knew that he made up rhymes.

This Sunday afternoon the good pair sat quietly when their son came running across the yard. In his excitement, he forgot his father, ran to his mother, and exclaimed, "Mother! I've seen it. I've seen it again. A beautiful horse! A beautiful horse in a cloud of golden dust. It stopped and looked at me!"

"What is this!?" Jacob was pale with rage and annoyance.

The child turned in sudden fear, but he had seen what he had seen, and he repeated that he had seen a beautiful horse in a cloud of golden dust. For this lie, he was sent indoors and set to read a chapter from the Bible.

Next Sunday, the family sat out under the oak tree once again. Little Paul went to the back of the house for a drink of water. He was gone a long time, and, when he did not answer her calls, Mrs. Heard went to look for him. Jacob Heard was angry, for he did not like his Sunday disturbed. He rose heavily from his chair and followed his wife.

The boy was looking up at his mother and saying, ". . . and he did, he stood there proud and pawing the earth and waiting for me. Truly, Mother, he is all golden. His tail and mane are silver."

Mrs. Heard only said, "Now quiet, Paul, quiet. You must not say such things."

But the boy went on, "And he let me ride him! We went over beautiful blue water and right over the mountains with their green trees, and up to the clouds. . . ."

"Thou liest!" thundered Jacob, pushing between the boy and his mother.

"No, Father. It's true!"

"Jacob, please Jacob," cried Mrs. Heard, for she recognized the black temper, and she moved in to protect her son.

Too late. Jacob raised his arm and struck the boy with his full strength. The child staggered and fell to the ground, blood pouring from nose and mouth. Jacob stood over him, shouting, "The boy is bewitched! A fiend has bewitched my child! Oh, God! Oh, God! Show me this fiend."

Mrs. Heard leaned over, picked up her unconscious boy, and, staggering under his weight, carried him into the cottage.

That night the child raved feverishly of his golden horse and of the beautiful places he saw from his back. Jacob, on one side of the bed, prayed for his soul, for the child was possessed. On the other side of the bed, the mother sat silently weeping, wiping the cold sweat from the child's brow as he turned and twisted, hour after hour, on through the night.

There was a moment near dawn when the child was suddenly quiet, and the mother and father both leaned over his bed. The child raised up and looked at them both and said calmly, "The horse is waiting for me. I can see the golden cloud."

Jacob looked at his child and then at his wife. He stood up, for in the night he thought he heard the pawing of a horse. Then his wife rose, and she too listened. "You hear?" she asked. And Jacob could not say that he did not. They looked at little Paul, and he too was listening. Then, with a cry of joy, he held out his arms, sank back, and was silent forever.

It was not yet dawn and Jacob walked slowly from his house. He thought the hoof beats were growing louder. A horse galloped into sight, came closer, and in the sudden white morning sun Jacob could see that its sides glowed like gold and its mane and tail were as silver. Jacob shrank back. A cloud of yellow dust enveloped the animal as it neared, then thundered past. On its back Jacob saw his boy, Paul.

It was then that remorse entered Jacob Heard, and a bitterness that was never to leave. Had not he, Jacob Heard, a pious man, just seen the vision for which he had struck his son? And in this vision and the shining face of little Paul he could not mistake the beauty of a godly thing.

Remembered

In a sermon on man's private and public life, Dr. Harry Emerson Fosdick once said that he, as an American, was very happy that George Washington did not allow his feelings for a certain lady, of whom he was alleged to have been enamored, to bring upon her any shame or even make her the object of gossip. This gave me a great interest in the unknown personal side of Washington's personality. The youthful Washington was strong, soldierly, and manly. But he was also, according to this legend, a man of great tenderness.

SHE moved with grace, and her gentleness and beauty were no less captivating because she wore dresses of leather, rode like the wind, and used a rifle better than most men about the country.

She lived with her great-grandfather, Old Abraham, at the point where the Youghiogheny and Monongahela Rivers join. These two were the sole survivors of an Indian raid that had wiped out their family. Marion kept the little cabin neat and clean, and provided food for the table by hunting and fishing. She spent much time reading to Old Abraham from his many books, for his eyes were unable to see the words he loved.

The small cabin was just off the trail along which General Braddock marched to his defeat. Marion and the old man had watched the gay-clad army pass, and had prayed they would defeat the Indians and bring peace to the countryside.

After the battle, the retreating army came back by the same route, and it was with sorrow that Marion watched them straggle by. The French and the Indians had ambushed General Braddock, who was unused to such unmilitary tactics.

Now during this retreat, and while Old Abraham was away from the cabin, Marion heard a knock at the door. She opened it to find an unprepossessing straggler of the defeated army before her, a bony-faced half-breed with red hair, whose name was Red Wolf. Seeing no one but the beautiful girl, he burst into the room. He would have tried not only to make free of the provisions of the little cabin but would have kissed the girl as well had she not leveled her rifle at him. Her steady eye and hand convinced Red Wolf of her courage, and he remained with upraised hands against the log wall. Finally, however, he began a slow movement toward her, his eyes holding hers— daring her to shoot a man in cold blood.

Her finger had tightened on the trigger when a young officer, in a silver-laced uniform, stepped through the open door and saved the situation. He doffed his three-cornered hat to the girl, and said sternly to Red Wolf, "Get gone. I will attend to you later."

Red Wolf slunk away through the door, and Washington, for it was he, apologized for the behavior of the soldier and begged that he might rest awhile in the pleasant little cottage.

Of course he was made most comfortable by the grateful girl and her great-grandfather. Marion's beauty, her grace, her innate refinement and gentleness did not fail to charm the young officer.

When Washington said goodbye to Marion the next day, he promised to return. He rode forward to find the remnants of his shattered army.

When the army disbanded, Washington rode back alone in haste, impatient to see Marion again. He found the little cabin in ashes. He called, but there was no answer. He walked about the ruins in sadness. Then he mounted his horse and galloped away. He put his hand inside his coat and felt, in the palm of his great hand, a silky lock of hair.

REMEMBERED

At Mt. Vernon, after Washington's death, there was found, folded in a piece of paper, a tress of brown hair. On the paper was written:

Marion, July 11, 1755.

Beautiful Doll

It is hard to kill a beautiful thing. I was hunting in Utah once, and after a time of tramping through the jack pine I came to a clearing. There stood a deer, and he was feeding. I raised my rifle to my shoulder and took aim. The deer raised his head, looked directly at me, stood motionless. Through the sight of my gun I beheld a creature so magnificent, so dignified, that the idea of shooting disappeared completely from my mind. I sensed only a feeling of wonderment as I gazed upon him. I felt ashamed and lowered the gun.

THE settlement of Fort Henry was located near the present city of Wheeling. The entire settlement was composed of fewer than twenty log cabins, crudely built with dirt floors and no windows. The furnishings in most of them consisted of a family bedstead and a few cherished dishes. The tables and chairs necessary for eating were fashioned out of rough wood and, while not very handsome, served their purpose well enough.

But handsome indeed was the wild, beautiful, near-virgin territory we now call West Virginia. Untouched forests and windswept hills shared sovereignty with the Indians who lived off the land, hunting and fishing for their food, hunting for the skins with which they clothed themselves.

Fort Henry itself was a former Indian trading post with a twenty-foot wall which had sharp wooden spikes along the top. There were no soldiers at the fort, which was used more for a meeting house than anything else. The local Indians were friendly and there seemed no need for fortifications.

Among the families in this clearing, there was one known to

men and women alike as the "beautiful doll." Her name was Elizabeth Zane and she was sixteen. Her face and figure still belonged to childhood. Her mouth was always merry, her laughter quick and sure.

In any other setting, wearing other clothes, she might have been a fairy princess, an inspiration to poets and painters. Even here in the wilderness, her beauty was such that it was respected and commented on by all. Even the children looked at her long blonde hair, blue eyes, and tiny hands and feet, and called her "doll."

This was the first year of the settlement and the twenty-odd families were having a difficult time. They had cleared their small tracts of land and had helped each other pull out tree stumps and remove the biggest rocks from the soil. At this winter's end they were pooling their food supplies and living frugally so as to be certain they could hold out till spring and the first planting. There were forty-two men doing the heavy work and a handful of strong women helping them. The rest tended to the lighter chores, raised the few animals, cooked the meals, and kept the children from straying. Elizabeth took care of the younger children.

Although it was February, the weather was balmy. Elizabeth and several of the smallest children played ring-around-the-rosy at the edge of the woods. Soon the children tired of the game and gathered around Elizabeth crying, "Tell us a story. Please tell us a story." They sat around her, one little boy cradled in her lap, the others under her arm or at her knee. The sun shone strongly on her blonde hair and created a halo around her head as the children in dirty calico sat quietly listening to her.

As she was telling her story, Elizabeth thought she noticed a slight movement behind one of the trees. Feeling that she was being watched, she still did not stop the story. Continuing, she lowered her eyes and suddenly raised them again. Her heart pounded as she thought she saw an Indian. Yes, she decided, it was an Indian—and wearing war paint at that.

She could not have known what the settlers later discovered: that only the heart-stirring sight of her beauty surrounded by children saved their lives.

Slowly and with infinite calm, for it was important to excite neither the children nor the savage behind the tree, Elizabeth, laughing and chattering, gathered her brood and walked them back to their mothers. Once in the settlement clearing, she went straight to her father and brothers and told them what she had seen.

Strangely enough, it was the women who declared that she had been seeing things. They had not seen anything. Nobody, they declared, had seen anything except Elizabeth Zane, and of course everybody knew what a daydreamer *she* was! However, because Elizabeth's father insisted, by nightfall the entire settlement was inside the fort. The women were grumbling, the men uneasy.

After supper Jonah Gibson took out his zither and began to sing "I Sowed the Seeds of Love," and it was obvious that he was singing it to Elizabeth. In the middle of the fourth verse his song was halted by a shriek. It was Mrs. Janeway, with an arrow in her arm!

Colonel Shepard, the only man in the colony who had ever led a military life, immediately assumed leadership. He posted the men with guns at intervals along the wall. Some of the women who could shoot received the remaining guns. The other women were given lookout posts or placed in a position to reload the guns as they were used.

There was no suspense and waiting for this Indian attack. Not more than a few minutes after the first arrow flew over the wall, a hailstorm of arrows came from all sides.

"There must be over a hundred," Shepard cried. "Pray God the powder holds out!"

The night wore on. One brave frontiersman after another fell under the rain of arrows. By midnight there were just twelve men and boys left of the forty-two who had been out felling trees that morning. The powder supply was just about gone.

"There's a powder keg in my brother's house," Elizabeth told Colonel Shepard.

"That's about a hundred feet from the west gate," said the Colonel. "Someone will have to make a run for it. It's our only possible chance."

Each of the remaining men stepped forward for the mission.

Then Elizabeth spoke up. "They did not harm me this afternoon. Perhaps I can get through—at least let me try. My life is not so important as the men we have left, who must fight for the children."

Before anyone could answer, she ran to the gate and slipped through. She walked out slowly, bathed in moonlight, a slow-moving target for even the poorest marksman. Once again, the very look of her seemed to hypnotize the bloodthirsty attackers. As those in the fort watched, she seemed to float to the door of her brother's cabin and out again carrying the powder keg.

Not until she was inches from safety did the spell she had created break. Spine-chilling cries filled the air and arrows flew about her. It was miraculous but they all missed her, and with a hop she was inside Fort Henry once more. Jonah Gibson, almost crying, took her in his arms.

Refreshed and inspired by Elizabeth's miraculous return, the remaining settlers fought with renewed vigor and tenacity. The disappointed Indians—probably tired, since what should have been an evening's sport had turned into a hard battle—picked up their wounded and disappeared.

Elizabeth married Jonah Gibson. Her children, knowing the story, would nod to each other years later when their Indian friends told them with awe about the snow-white apparition whose glowing beauty had made them powerless, for a while, to shoot their arrows.

Mr. X and the Loyalty Oath

*They say you can't teach an old dog new tricks—and it's
also mighty hard to make an eccentric old man change
his politics. This might be a shocking story except for
the fact that Mr. X, the crotchety old man, had an
equally crotchety sense of humor.*

W E WILL call the main character of this tale Mr. X,
because the family of this old Tory are still a little
touchy about the matter, or so I'm told. I don't
know why, for it was a long time ago.

Mr. X lived in Lenox, Massachusetts, during the Revolutionary War. He was quite wealthy and of a prominent family.
These two assets gave him immunity during early Revolutionary days, even though he was wont to call the rebellion "madness," drink the health of the king, and speak contemptuously
of Mr. Washington and the other Whigs.

Most of the citizens of Lenox were very pro-Whig, and
when the Battle of Bunker Hill was over, feelings ran high.
Mr. X, however, did not spare the Whigs his comments. Perhaps this would not have been so bad, but when Mr. X was
allowed to express his opinions, several other Tories followed
suit. The Whigs, watching the trend of things, decided it was
bad for morale, so a committee was organized and they called
Mr. X to account. They told Mr. X very plainly that he must
stop all this nonsense and swear allegiance to the Colonies.
Because he was an old and established citizen, they gave him
the choice of two alternatives: return to England or be hanged.

Mr. X was no coward. He told them in no uncertain terms
that he was not going to England, that he had been born in
Massachusetts and that, by gad, he intended to stay in Massachusetts!

To make a long story short, they hung him.

73

There was a ready-made gallows on the square at Lenox. They pulled the old boy up and let him hang—for a minute. Then they let him down, and after a hooker of rum was administered, he came around. He was offered the oath. He refused, by gad, and told them to proceed with the business at hand.

Now the good citizens of Lenox who had grown up with Mr. X had not figured on this. They thought that when their old friend felt the noose tighten, he would change his politics. When he didn't, they gave him another upward ride—this time with a pretty quick jerk. The old man hung there dangling, a little blue in the face. When his eyeballs began to bulge, it was obviously time to let him down, because nobody wanted to kill the old buzzard; they just wanted to teach him some sense. Down he came, and this time it took quite awhile to bring him to. Again Mr. X was offered the oath.

He merely grunted, "To h--- with Washington and all the Whigs!"

This time they hoisted the old boy heavenward in a manner that was very businesslike. Soon Mr. X's eyes were out even farther than before, and his color was rather more black than the blue of before. Indeed it looked as if it were all over, when somebody noticed a faint signal from his hand and they let him down again. He couldn't talk, for the throat is a delicate instrument and cannot take such punishment repeatedly. They brought him a piece of paper and asked him again whether he'd take the oath. "I'll swear," he penned, or perhaps they said "quilled" in those days.

With a shout of joy and a great deal of relief the crowd carried Mr. X to the local tavern. He was seated before the hearth, given a bowl of punch, and when he had recovered his voice, he gave a toast to the health of General Washington and the assembled Whigs. Many a jolly bowl later, he was heard to roar: "Down with the king," and everybody was happy indeed.

Next day, after Mr. X had recovered from the liquefaction of the night before, he was heard to say, "It's a d⊄ʒ⊄ ⧜d hard way to make a Whig, but it'll do it."

An Unsung Heroine

The songs of wars celebrate the generals, the commanders, and the heroic men of combat. Yet I suspect that it is the collective deeds of many little people which play an important part as well. So let us sing of Mrs. Darrah!

I T ISN'T often that a middle-aged woman can save an army and perhaps a nation. This is the story of one who did— and by the oft-scorned feminine weakness of listening through a keyhole.

Mrs. Lydia Darrah, forty-five and widowed by the War of Independence, was in bed on a cold winter's night, only too typical of December in Philadelphia. With the shortage of firewood, bed was the only place to keep warm and then under a mountain of comforters.

Mrs. Darrah was not to be snug for long. She was roused by a knock on her door and when she went to answer it, there were four British officers standing courteously. They removed their hats as she appeared and their spokesman said, "May we trouble you once again, ma'am, for the use of your back chamber? We are, as always, grateful for your co-operation and hope we will not be too much disturbing you."

Mrs. Darrah beckoned them in without a word. In order to save her house, she had compromised her principles and had offered the British her extra room for billeting soldiers. They had not accepted her offer, but had instead made her home a center for their secret conferences, away from headquarters. They often disturbed her at odd hours of the night and at such times, she would shake her head disapprovingly but keep silent.

The four men removed their cloaks and, bowing to Mrs. Darrah, walked quietly into the back parlor which had become their conference room. Mrs. Darrah returned to bed, but the

77

sound of their voices would not let her rest. Her curiosity prodded her from her warm resting place. In her bed socks, she crept stealthily down the stairs to the closed parlor door. All she could hear were murmuring voices but no separate words. Mrs. Darrah felt no shame in kneeling and putting her good left ear next to the keyhole.

". . . Major Martin marches in two days from the north. You, Captain Green—look here on this map—will flank his attack from this point. Gentlemen, we can surround White Marsh so completely that General Washington would have to be a conjurer to escape."

"Gentlemen, if we succeed and capture Washington, the war is over. We can all go home to our wives."

Mrs. Darrah did not wait to hear more, but quietly tiptoed back to her chamber, anxiety and fear accelerating her heartbeat. Her fear was not only for the American Army at White Marsh but for her own son. She had only one boy, and he was at that moment on special duty with General Washington at White Marsh.

It seemed many hours later that the British finally left the house. Mrs. Darrah did not sleep. Again and again she rehearsed this possibility and that. She had to do something to warn the Americans.

At breakfast, Mrs. Darrah casually announced to her two daughters, "Now what do you think, my dears? We have run out of flour. I will go to Frankfurt today and get some from the mill."

"It isn't safe," Dorothy, the younger daughter, replied.

"Oh, Mother will be safe enough if she takes a servant," replied Armina, the older girl. "It wouldn't be safe to be on the roads alone, with soldiers everywhere."

Mrs. Darrah laughed at her children and allayed their fears, "What would soldiers want with a middle-aged woman? I shall go alone."

"But Frankfurt is beyond the British lines. How will you get through?"

"Why, General Howe will give me a pass. He will not refuse me—he knows I have co-operated with his officers."

General Howe had spent a pleasant night, first at the theater, and then with his mistress. He was in great, good humor and bowed deeply when Mrs. Darrah greeted him and smiled coyly. He gave her the pass and a warning, "Be careful, madam, of snipers. This pass will permit you through the lines, but alas will not give you a charmed life."

Mrs. Darrah thanked him and went her way. She passed safely through the lines, and then urged her horse through Frankfurt at a fast gallop. She reached the mill and left her flour bags with the miller. "I shall return in an hour," she said. "The British keep us so closely that neither the horse nor myself has had any exercise for days. I'm going to give him a good run."

On approaching the American lines, Mrs. Darrah found herself blocked by an American patrol. "Halt!" Two men were standing on either side of the road, rifles fixed. Mrs. Darrah stopped, puzzled at what to do next.

"I am Lydia Darrah of Philadelphia, and I have come to see my son Edward who is serving General Washington."

The men were not to be taken in by this. "How did you get through the British lines?" asked one. "She's obviously a British spy," declared the other, as he took the reins from her hands. "You will be detained, madam, but do not fear bodily harm. General Washington does not shoot lady spies."

"But I've only come to see my poor fatherless son," the good patriot cried in anguish, as they led her toward the encampment. There was nothing she could do, so she allowed them to lead her horse.

What was her joy on seeing a familiar face just as the men were requiring her to dismount. "Colonel Craig! Colonel Craig, please!"

The officer turned. "Why, Mrs. Darrah," he exclaimed. "Whatever are you doing here at White Marsh?"

The good lady was in tears, "Oh, they think I'm a spy,

Colonel Craig, and I'm a prisoner. Please, if I could only speak to you alone for one moment, dear Colonel Craig, I think I could convince you that it is only my son who has brought me here."

Colonel Craig hesitated only a minute. "You can release this lady into my custody," he ordered the patrol. "I will be personally responsible for her."

He assisted Mrs. Darrah in dismounting, then led her into one of the nearby tents. Here he made her sit down before he would let her tell her story. He had to promise the overwrought lady that he would keep what she told him in strictest confidence except to General Washington. He promised more because he had known her husband than because he attached any importance to what she was going to say.

"I listened in at the door and the British are none the wiser," she said. "I cannot jeopardize my home and children, Colonel, you understand that, so the British must never know it was I informed on them. You see, I planned to find my son and have him tell General Washington. The British are planning a surprise attack on White Marsh day after tomorrow!"

"Are you sure about this?"

"Yes, and they said Major Martin and Captain Green would be attacking, and that General Washington could not escape."

Colonel Craig rose and assisted the lady to her feet. "You have much courage, Mrs. Darrah. Do not fear. I will take the proper steps. Go now and return to Philadelphia immediately. My man will take you safely to the American lines, my dangerous spy. Be sure that when the redcoats make their surprise attack tomorrow, they are the ones who will be surprised."

Mrs. Darrah arrived back in Philadelphia late that afternoon, two heavy sacks of flour strapped on either side of her saddle. Her daughters greeted her with relief and Dorothy cried fondly, "I see you got what you were after, Mother dear."

"Yes, child, I did," answered Mrs. Darrah, smiling wearily. "How tired I am."

The Heroine of the
Mohawk Valley

*Faced with an emergency people will do the darndest
things. I can remember when I was helping to fight
a brushfire in California and we suddenly saw a rattlesnake, coiled and hissing, alone on top of a rock
surrounded by a ring of fire. It seemed the most
natural thing in the world, at the time, to get a long
pole, with which to reach it through the flames, and
to see that it got safely away. It was not till afterward
that all of us remembered the times we had killed
rattlesnakes. Now this story has nothing to do with
snakes, but it does make me realize that in an emergency people will do the darndest things.*

THE Mohawk Valley of New York State is today a para-
dise of rolling hills, fertile and prosperous farms, and
above all has an air of quiet repose. The original settlers
in this valley were primarily Dutch descendents of the original
colonists of lower New York, and English families from the
Massachusetts Bay Colony. Members of both national groups
were basically alike: brave, steadfast, hardy, dedicated to home
and family, determined to create a new, productive life for
themselves in the valley. This they were able to do, for the
Mohawk Indians proved their friendliness and showed a peace-
loving temperament. Yet all this quiet of the present and the
past was disturbed during the time of the Revolutionary War.

Sir John Johnston was one of many military leaders sent from
London by George III to subdue evidence of revolution in
whatever way he thought best. As part of an over-all plan of
demoralization, Sir John enlisted the aid of Mohawk Indians
by inciting their hatred of the settlers and offering them ammunition with which to destroy the intruders. He pointed out

to them that all the rich farms of the few hundred inhabitants would then belong to the Indians. He promised to support them if intruders once again came into their land.

He might have succeeded had it not been for Nancy Van Alstine.

At forty-seven Nancy was a well-built, handsome woman of quick movement, ready wit, and a talent for getting things done. In her twenty-nine years of marriage to Martin Van Alstine she had given birth to fifteen children, all of whom were alive and as vivacious as their mother. Her home, the Van Alstine mansion, set on the banks of the Mohawk River, was the oldest and most beautiful in the valley. It was a century old, having been built by the first Van Alstines who moved upstate from New Amsterdam.

In the summer of 1780, August to be exact, the War of Independence had not made much impact on the Mohawk Valley. In this month the Indians began to make raid after raid on the valley inhabitants, killing many and firing their fields and homes.

Mrs. Van Alstine went about her chores in her usual cool way, outwardly unmoved. One morning when she was working in her kitchen garden she heard the sound of galloping hooves. She had not been on her feet a moment when her nearest neighbor, Peter Vanderhooven, rode up and leaped off his mount.

"Get your brood together, Nancy!" he gasped. "The Mohawks are crazy up the valley. They burned the Farrington farm and it will be my house next and then yours. Give me a drink from your pump, and I'll be off to warn every farm this end of the valley!"

The frightened matron ran quickly to the pump and drew a cup of water for the parched man. While he drank, she cupped her hands about her mouth and called out the names of each of her fifteen children. In reporting the story, Peter declared that she called so loudly that it made him cringe.

"Children," Nancy announced when they had dutifully gathered around her, "the Indians are coming to take us, and I want you to know that I expect each of you to be brave. As an example to the others, of course."

"What others, Mama?" the youngest asked.

"Your older brothers and sisters are going to fetch the neighbors right now, and we are all going to hide out on the island till the trouble blows over. No sense anyone getting killed if we can help it."

From where Mrs. Van Alstine stood she could see past her children the island that she and her husband owned in the middle of the Mohawk River. Not a very big island, it served for picnics and summertime camp-outs for the children. Now its tiny shack would be handy for helping to feed thirty or forty neighbor women and their young. She sent the older children off to bring the neighbors to this island retreat with youngsters, bedding, and cooking pots.

Although Nancy Van Alstine probably would not have admitted it, it was apparent that she secretly enjoyed the emergency and her ability to outsmart the enemy.

While her children were out rounding up the neighbors, she set to work making as many meat pies as the stove would hold. She pulled out great sacks of flour and carried beef from the smokehouse into the kitchen to make more pies. As the last bubbling pie came out of the brick oven, she could hear wagons arriving and the shouts of her neighbors.

One by one they loaded their bedding and what foodstuffs they could into the Van Alstine barge. Two of the boys rowed it back and forth to the island. Five trips in all completed the task. Since the weather was fine the children cavorted as though it were a picnic, and the mothers set about sharing the work and making themselves as comfortable as possible.

A lookout was kept on the shore. And next morning they could see fire at the Farrington house. Not much later they could see Indians arriving at the Van Alstine mansion. Strangely enough and much to the relief of Nancy, the Indians, finding nobody at home, left and in no way molested the house.

With the passing of another day the picnic spirit wavered, and the women watched the shore with wonder and fear. As another day passed and there was no sign of the Indians returning, several trips to the shore started each mother and her brood for home. As each group left they hardly exchanged farewells for each dreaded the sight that might await them at their own home.

Nancy Van Alstine entered her own house as if she had merely been away for a vacation.

Early the next morning as she sat at breakfast with her family, the front door flew open and several savage-looking Mohawks entered. They did not disturb the family nor did they speak. Wordlessly they began to move the furniture out of the house piece by piece. Nancy could not remain quiet.

"What do you think you are doing," she demanded imperiously, in her most frightening tone.

"Mother, stop, they will kill us," her oldest son cautioned.

He was too late. Nancy sprang at the nearest Indian, tearing the chair he was carrying out of his hand. He pulled his knife but did not use it. Nancy subsided against the wall. The Indian stood over her, knife poised. She dared not interfere again while the other raiders carried off every movable object in the house, including pots, pans, clothing and bedclothes.

The final humiliation came when one of the Indians caught sight of the richly embroidered flowers on Nancy Van Alstine's gown and tried to rip them off. He succeeded merely in tearing the front panel thus exposing the first of the eight petticoats the lady wore.

Looking from her doorway she watched the Mohawks tie her three milk cows to the loaded wagon and lead them away. For the first time since her husband had gone off to war, Mrs. Van Alstine cried.

With fifteen children and no furniture, no woolens or bedding to keep them warm, no cows to give them milk, no cooking utensils to prepare their meals and keep them healthy, she was in a desperate way. For three weeks she struggled without blankets and without pots. Then suddenly her tears gave way to annoyance and finally her annoyance to righteous indignation.

"Who do these godless creatures think they are?" she asked her children.

They knew better than to answer her when she was in such a mood.

"Son," she addressed her oldest boy of fifteen, "fetch the horse and pull out the sleigh. We will grease the sleigh runners so the horse can pull it along the dirt road. You and I are going to pay a call on the Mohawks!"

The Indian camp was eighteen miles up the valley from the Van Alstine house. It was a permanent settlement of rude wooden houses and small garden plots. Mrs. Van Alstine who was riding the lead horse slipped off as they arrived and strode into the biggest of the houses. A woman sat on the hard-packed earth floor. There were no men in the camp since they were out hunting game. Without addressing the Indian woman, Nancy unceremoniously grabbed up anything that was hers. Armful after armful she loaded onto the sleigh until it was full. Tethered in one of the gardens were cows. She untied the three that were hers and walked them quickly to the sleigh. She and her son greased the runners again, tied the cows to the back of the sleigh, and returned home as fast as they could. That night the Van Alstine's ate a good supper and slept snugly in their warm beds.

At dawn galloping horses shattered the quiet. The Indians in full war dress, armed with tomahawks and rifles, rode up to the house and dismounted. From the window the watching Nancy saw two of them go toward the stable.

"My precious cows," she thought, and rushed from the house, still clad in her dressing gown, her thick brown hair in braids.

"Stop, stop," she commanded as she thrust herself in front of the Indians at the stable door. "You cannot take my cows again!"

"You stole them from us while we hunted for food," said one Mohawk stepping forward.

"I stole back what was mine, only what you stole from me weeks ago," she replied.

The Indian raised his rifle and pointed it at her.

"Shoot if you dare," Mrs. Van Alstine cried and tearing open her dressing gown, she exposed her neck and chest.

Now the Mohawks were a tribe who preferred hunting and fishing to fighting in any case. What is more they had known the Van Alstines for many years. Whatever the cause, the sight of this woman shamed the Mohawk and his companions, and they turned and left.

It is a matter of record that Nancy Van Alstine was not molested again. She lived to be ninety-eight and on that day she received many congratulations and messages of praise—one from the very Indian she had dared to shoot her. A prosperous farmer and tribal leader by then, the Indian said, "If there had been fifty such women as Nancy Van Alstine in the Mohawk Valley, the Indians would never have dared to molest the farmers. Without her the valley would even now be suffering the desolation of our folly."

EPILOGUE

A Mohawk Valley historian wrote in 1835, "The war whoop of the cruel Mohawk sounds no more from the forest ambush; the dews and rains have washed away the red stains on the soft sward, and green and peaceful in the sunshine lies the tomb of Nancy Van Alstine, the embodiment of American womanhood."

Love and War

"Love, it is a funny thing"—and it is as strong as the lovers involved. The affection which can make a man come through enemy lines to spend an evening with his beloved is not only romance but adventure. I find great charm in young Lewis Morris, who loved Anne Elliott of New York, and would see her no matter what.

I T WAS wartime, during the American Revolution, to be exact, and Anne Elliott was in love. Despite the fact that New York was occupied by the British Howe, despite the many doubts that the Colonies would win, she was in love and the world was wonderful.

The Elliotts lived in a red brick house with white shutters and white doors just north of Bowling Green. Though, with the other Whigs, they lived in a city overrun by redcoats, the atmosphere of the city was not that of a defeated people. Perhaps it was only Anne who thought this for, after all, battles were fought on the battlefield, and the British troops were always gracious and courteous to ladies, especially pretty ones.

Not quite twenty-two years old, dark-haired, blue-eyed, and ivory-skinned, Anne Elliott was betrothed to Colonel Lewis Morris, of General Washington's army. Colonel Morris was a handsome man with large uneven features, and a head of thick unruly hair which with great difficulty he kept tied back in a ribbon. It was a matter of great wonder to Anne how a man who was such a splendid figure as a soldier, who was a leader of fighting men, could be at the same time such a gentle suitor, a tender lover, and a pasionate claimant of her heart.

But he was, she thought joyously, and what was more there was tucked in her bodice on this day a tiny scrap of paper with

91

no signature—as if she did not know the handwriting! The scrap of paper said he would be coming to see her tonight in disguise, and hang the British!

Major Elliott, Anne's father, was in Pennsylvania recruiting men. Her mother had been away for two days tending to Marissa Higgins, who expected a baby at any moment. That left only Mrs. Drew, the cook, in the house besides Anne. Mrs. Drew had been in the Elliott household for twenty years and could be counted upon for discretion.

Anne rushed to the kitchen and hugged the cook warmly, announcing, "We're having a secret visitor tonight, Mrs. Drew. I can't tell you his name but his favorite dish is kidney pie. If you love me, you'll make the best kidney pie between here and Yorkshire."

The cook's face clouded. "I hope your young man is right coming in here," she said. "The Black Dragoons are patrolling and troublemakers they are, too. Stopped me this morning to look in my shopping basket. Said I might have gunpowder hidden under the sugar! Near frightened me to death, they did, stopping me and searching me in the middle of Bowling Green!"

"You never mind, Mrs. Drew. Don't you worry about it. Just make the best kidney pie ever you have made. Colonel Morris is clever . . . and careful. He'll come in a wonderful disguise, and I wouldn't be surprised if he showed up in a Dragoon's uniform or dressed up as George the Third."

The girl fairly skipped from the kitchen into the dining room and began to set the table. Her mother would be furious, but none the less Anne pulled out the very best table-cloth, which had taken her mother over ten years to embroider. Smiling and singing to herself, she placed upon it the Sheffield silver cutlery, the heirloom goblets, and the gold-plate china. She finished it off with a centerpiece of roses and violets from the garden.

Satisfied for the moment with the dining room, Anne went to her bedroom, rolled her hair into rag curlers and lay down for a nap. She wanted to be bright-eyed and rosy-cheeked for her Lewis. Despite excitement and anticipation she went off to sleep immediately, after reminding herself severely that time passes most quickly in slumber.

Mrs. Drew awakened her for afternoon tea. Anne jumped from bed, unrolled her hair and brushed it till it shone. She wound it and rolled it over her fingers strand by strand into a series of long curls. These she tied in two separate bunches behind each ear, fastening them in place with little combs. She selected a red and gold silk dress because Lewis had often admired it. A white cashmere shawl from France which belonged to her mother finished her costume. While dressing thus, she listened attentively for any sound which would announce her fiancé's arrival. Nothing. Finally dressed, she looked at her image in the mirror from all angles and, satisfied, went downstairs to the sitting room. Waiting was the most difficult part. She picked up her needlework and threw it down. She tried to read . . . the words stared back at her. She went to the pianoforte and attempted to play.

Suddenly she jumped up! Was that the back door? She raced through the kitchen into the pantry, where Mrs. Drew at the door was asking, "Who is it?"

A voice from outside replied, "The baker's boy, ma'am, with the bread."

"Hmpf!" Mrs. Drew retorted, "Go away. I ordered no bread. You are mistaken."

But Anne uttered a shriek. "No! No! Let him in, Mrs. Drew! No, let me . . ." and she threw open the door. There, to all outward intent, was the baker's boy, wearing homespun and apron, with a handcart of bread.

He bowed low when he saw the fine lady. "Your bread made to order," he said.

"Dear lad, you must be tired," Anne condescended, "step into our kitchen for a moment and rest yourself."

This the baker's boy did. Once the door was closed, he swept the blushing girl into his arms. Mrs. Drew bustled

93

around for a moment, then withdrew into the dining room to hide her embarrassment.

"I can't stay long, my darling," Colonel Morris said, "but seeing you is enough to sustain me during the winter."

"We're having your favorite dish, kidney pie," Anne announced irrelevantly. "Oh, come into the sitting room. Tell me what you've been doing every single minute!"

"You are more beautiful than ever, Anne," he whispered, ignoring her request. "I am the most fortunate man in the New World—and the old one, too, for that matter."

When Mrs. Drew announced dinner was ready, time and war were forgotten as the happy couple ate, and drank each other's health in common brown ale. Mrs. Drew served them coffee in the sitting room where Anne played the pianoforte and Colonel Morris sang to her accompaniment.

Suddenly there was a loud rapping at the front door! With what terror they listened at the sitting room door as Mrs. Drew called through the front entrance, "Who is it?"

The answer came loudly and strongly, "Dragoon patrol, madam! We have information a rebel officer is in your house. We intend to search."

Mrs. Drew was quick-witted, "You have no warrant," she retorted.

"Open up! Need I remind you we are at war and control this area. Open up!"

"My mistress is sleeping. Let me wake her first." Mrs. Drew motioned Anne and her lover upstairs as she spoke.

Anne whispered to Mrs. Drew to stay beside the door, and she and Colonel Morris ran up the stairs. In her bedroom, Anne threw her most voluminous dressing gown over her dress. She loosened her hair, tousled it with her fingers. Turning down her bedspread, she crushed the pillow and ruffled up the sheets. Then the helpless Colonel Morris was shoved into the clothes closet behind her ball gowns and cautioned not to breathe at all.

94

A sleepy Anne appeared at the head of the stairs and called to Mrs. Drew. "Let in whoever it is," she directed sleepily.

Mrs. Drew opened the door, and a tall, stern-faced Black Dragoon captain strode in. At the top of the stairs, Anne yawned sleepily again and dropped her eyes. "Why do you get me out of bed, Captain?" she inquired, all sleepiness, courtesy, and respect.

"We have been informed that a certain colonial officer, your betrothed, will secretly visit this house tonight."

The young girl was suddenly all awake and beaming with happiness. "Captain," she cried, "is this true? Oh, I must dress myself and not allow him to see me in such wretched condition."

The stern-faced Dragoon smiled. He could not help it. "What a beautiful rebel you are. Tell me, pray, why you are in bed so early?"

"I was not well, sir, and had hoped to avoid a greater illness by means of rest."

"Do not let this visit disturb your rest, lovely lady, for if it is this colonial's intention to visit your house, we will intercept him, to be sure. In the meantime, good night—we shall not disturb you further."

At the head of the stairs Anne curtsied to him.

The captain bowed. "Good night, Miss Elliott. When we have put down this foolish rebellion, perhaps you will allow me the pleasure of calling on you."

"Of course, Captain," Anne flirted with him, "when you put the rebellion down."

Dragoons patrolled the house until dawn. Although no one slept within the house, not a sound emerged. But next morning the Dragoons had been called to other duty and a well-fed baker's assistant slipped out the back door and pushed his cart through the winding streets.

Adventuring

How many people have had the experience as a child of being completely alone in the quiet of the woods where the only sounds are birds and the stealthy rustlings of innumerable unseen creatures? Even today I imagine that most children have had an illusion like this once or twice. But it is an illusion. For children of today, even those fortunate enough to have a forest to wander in, know that it's only a matter of time before they will see a ranger's tower or a curl of industrial smoke. They know that beyond the forest lies a town. The children of 1750 did not know this. They knew that beyond the forest lay . . . more forest; they knew that in the forest lurked many dangers, and that stealthy rustlings could mean more than a wary rabbit, could mean the presence of an enemy Indian. Many boys of that time grew up in this environment and chose it as their way of life, a way of life filled with the enchantment of silence, freedom, and adventure.

LEWIS WETZEL was born in 1764, on the Big Wheeling, in Virginia.

Daniel Boone was born in 1734 near what is now the town of Reading, Pennsylvania.

The homes in which these lads were born were practically identical. The cabins, which were built of felled logs, must have approximated twenty by sixteen feet. The floors were bare earth or puncheons (logs split into planks and then laid on the ground). The cabins were constructed by rolling up the logs layer by layer. Each log was put into place, notched, and then fitted at the corners. Two whole trees were then set up on both of the short sides of the rectangle of the house. The branches were trimmed so that their height was even and formed a V to support a cross pole, and a roof made of sheets of bark was put on and held in place by a log. Clay and mud filled the space between the logs to keep out the cold. The interior was one room which served all purposes. These cabins were built in forest clearings on the edge of a boundless tract of untouched wilderness.

Young Daniel spent his childhood hunting and dreaming in the woods with their fish-filled streams, game—and hostile Indians. He became as much a part of wood life as the very animals that lived around him. He had a love of physical action among the trees, and acquired remarkable skill in woodcraft. Young Lewis Wetzel learned his craft in the same natural way.

When Daniel was ten years old, he disappeared from home. Frantic parents and neighbors searched the forest for him to no avail. The searching party was three days out and ready to give up when one of the men saw a column of smoke in the distance. Fearful that it was made by Indians who had captured Daniel, the men approached cautiously. Standing behind trees, they saw a primitive cabin made of tree limbs, brush, and grass sods piled together. One of the men quietly moved closer until he could see inside. There were no Indians. Inside sat Daniel, with his dog, contentedly cooking choice pieces of meat from animals he had shot and skinned in the last three days. Daniel was amazed at their concern. He returned home willingly enough, promising only that he would tell them the next time he decided to repeat the exploit.

At the age of ten, Lewis Wetzel had a much more realistic experience. His cabin home was attacked by Indians. His mother and the younger children escaped, but Lewis and his brother Jacob, two years younger, were taken away as prisoners. The boys were so young that their captors did not bother to bind them. At night while the Indians slept, Lewis led his younger brother from the camp. When they were safely behind trees, however, Lewis stopped and declared that he did not like the idea of returning home barefooted. He decided to go back and get moccasins for himself and Jacob. This he did.

"We can't get along without a gun," he said on returning; "wait here a little longer and I'll bring one back." This, too, he did.

Thus moccasined and armed, Lewis discovered the homeward trail. Knowing they would be pursued, he kept watch and when the Indians approached on their trail, hid himself and his brother until they passed. The youngsters reached Wheeling by the middle of the next day, constructed a raft, and crossed the river.

When the ten-year-old boy reached home, he found the cabin a smoldering ruin and in it the charred body of his father. He and his brother were shaken and filled with fury. With every phrase that their young minds could remember from the Bible, they vowed that as long as they lived they would kill every Indian that it was in their power to kill. And so they did.

It was the fortune of these young men to be a part of the penetration and settling of that area of Virginia which we now know as Kentucky and Tennessee. Both of these men had similar experiences with the Indians of that area. Both of them went into the Kentucky region because it offered them an opportunity to use their woodcraft and to live in the best way they knew how.

One can picture them as they were in the period of the Revolutionary War: each in a hunting shirt of dressed deerskins, and leggings and moccasins of the same strong material; their trousers fringed down the seams after the fashion of the Southern Indians; their undergarments of cotton so coarse as to seem like the sackcloth of our day; each carrying as a matter of course a powder horn, rifle, hatchet and bullet pouch. These would be all the tools they would need—other than their bravery and knowledge—to face the loneliness, the menace, the privations, and the bountifulness of the Kentucky wilderness.

FIRST HUNTER OF KENTUCKY

In the middle of the eighteenth century, that part of the Virginia territory's forests which we now call Kentucky was hardly known to white men. At this time and for years afterward, this forest was regarded by the Indians as a neutral hunting ground, to which no particular tribe could lay claim. Each tribe had equal rights to hunt, but when members of various tribes encountered one another there, they would wage deadly hand-to-hand battles. They united only against their common enemy, the interloping white man.

Young Daniel Boone was married at the age of twenty and settled in the Yadkin Valley of North Carolina, where he made a living by hunting and trapping. In his thirty-fourth year a party of hunters en route to Kentucky stopped at his home. From them Daniel heard of the deer, the bison, the wild turkeys, the numerous well-stocked streams of the unknown territory. He learned, too, that in Kentucky there were no settlements and that a man could live there in freedom. These tales filled him with restlessness; he could not resist his desire to see this land. Avowing to his wife that the country of "Kaintuck" might offer the whole family (he had five children by this time) greater opportunities, he joined the party of hunters.

Thus there started out for Kentucky a hunting party made up of John Finley, James Moncey, John Stuart, William Cool, and Daniel Boone. Daniel was a welcome addition to the party because of his recognized prowess in the forests.

Under Daniel's guidance, they traveled fast and in a month had climbed the steep slope of a mountain that bordered their destination. When they reached the top, they could see hundreds of miles stretched out before them, valleys and hills laced by streams, forests alternating with natural clearings. They could see level country upon which millions of bison seemed to be moving, and their watchful eyes actually observed deer and other wild animals, roaming in freedom because only an occasional redman came to disturb their peace.

The hunters decided that they could not light their campfire on the mountaintop; to do so would be to announce their presence for many miles over the wilderness. Although there had been no evidence of Indians, Daniel was too cautious to take the chance of being seen. He moved his party downhill to camp for the night in a ravine.

The spot Daniel chose was near a huge tree that had been uprooted by a recent storm. He made the trunk of this tree the rear wall of the camp, piled logs and brush on two other sides, and left the fourth side open. On the open side, Finley kindled a fire against another small log. Thus secured against chill and wild animals, they passed their first night on the Kentucky side in well-deserved rest.

All through the summer and autumn the men explored an ever-widening area. They worked out of their original camp, which they had made permanent by adding a roof to keep out the rain. From here they hunted bison, wild turkeys, bear, and other game. By the end of autumn they had accumulated many skins and had a thorough knowledge of many miles of territory. They had never seen an Indian and had practically decided that none ever entered this part of the land.

It was in December that their peace was rudely shattered. The men went out hunting in pairs, and Daniel and John Stuart often hunted together. They hunted the buffalo, which were so numerous and so unused to being hunted that they could be approached very closely. One evening they were following a buffalo path on their way back to camp, walking along through the cane with no thought of concealment, when they reached a small hill near the Kentucky river and began the ascent to camp.

Indians suddenly sprang from the canebrake! Caught at a complete disadvantage, the two men surrendered and were immediately disarmed. The Indians did not respond to any of their attempts to talk, and Boone and Stuart decided that the language of these savages must be completely different from any others they had known. They decided, too, that they would try to escape at the first opportunity. Their hands were kept bound, and they were under constant surveillance. Both men pretended complete indifference to their fate and such willingness to learn from the Indians that by the seventh day of their captivity, Daniel and Stuart were freed from their bonds. But they were still constantly watched.

On this seventh day, the two white men hunted successfully with the Indians and partook of the savages' evening meal. That night, with the others, they stretched out on the ground, rolled in their blankets with their feet pointing toward the fire. Daniel, ever alert, watched the Indian who had been guarding him and noticed that for the first time the hunter was inattentive and drowsy. Daniel could not communicate this to Stuart, but as those around them dropped off to sleep he remained alert and watchful. At midnight Daniel raised his head. All were asleep . . . Stuart was asleep! Stuart was sleeping, in fact, as soundly as the Indians, and Daniel could not think of a way to awaken him that would not also mean waking the lightly sleeping savages. Yet he could not go away alone. With infinite care, Daniel inched toward Stuart and touched his face. Fortunately, his friend awoke without a start. Conversation was unnecessary.

The fire had burned low. The logs smoldered as two noiseless figures moved out of the dim light into the darkness and thence into the forest.

Although they were seven days from their camp, they unerringly set off in its general direction, guiding themselves by the stars as well as by the feel of tree barks. They did not halt in the darkness and by morning were in country which they recognized. They pressed on quickly and finally were at their original camp site.

Imagine their consternation on finding the camp deserted. They could not tell from the signs whether their friends had been slain by Indians or had themselves razed the little edifice. They consulted together about their best course of action. Their ammunition was running low and they admitted to each other that they were anxious for word from their families back home. There didn't seem to be much purpose in remaining in this already explored area, yet if their friends had returned to North Carolina believing them dead, their share of the skins would have long since been divided between the others. Therefore, the two men reasoned, it would be more practical to remain here in the Kentucky forest yet a while than return home with nothing to show for their adventure.

They did not dare stay at the site of their original camp, knowing that the Indians from whom they had escaped would be searching for them. Such was the ingenuity of Daniel and Stuart, so great their skill and patience in moving to a new camp site each day, that they were able to completely elude the Indians during the next few months they remained in the forest.

One day, returning from a day's hunting to that spot where they were storing their new accumulation of skins, Daniel and Stuart thought they heard voices. Immediately taking cover behind trees, they waited and were surprised to see two white hunters emerge from among the trees. After watching the newcomers awhile, Daniel suddenly ran out crying, "Squire! Squire!"

He had recognized his younger brother, Squire, who with a companion had come to search for Daniel and discover his fate. This search had been inspired by the return to Carolina of Finley and the other hunters, who, as Daniel and Stuart had expected, assumed they were dead and had so informed their families. Squire Boone, however, refused to believe that the forest could conquer his brother Daniel, and this faith had motivated his journey to Kentucky. The brothers' joy at their reunion was unparalleled. Moreover, in addition to bringing news of their families and friends, the newcomers also brought badly needed ammunition, and all four decided to stay together and hunt.

The Indians were quiet, but there was evidence that they were still searching for Stuart and Daniel Boone. Late one afternoon, when Daniel and his friend were standing beside a bison they had just killed, they were suddenly fired upon by a party of Indians. Stuart dropped dead. Daniel raced into the forest, and hidden by the trees he watched the scalping of the dead Stuart. This left only three white hunters.

Another day the Boone brothers were hunting together and when they returned to camp found that the companion they had left behind had disappeared. They made an intensive search for him, but he had left no sign. The brothers debated about the wisdom of returning home. Daniel hankered a bit for his wife and children, but life in the forest satisfied him as no other could. The brothers finally decided that Squire would go on and Daniel remain to hunt for a period.

Daniel lived alone in the forest for three months, his life spiced by those who tracked him and those whom he tracked. As active as his enemies, as much a master of woodcraft as they, he kept out of the way of the Indians while at the same time he was also searching for them. He and the savages played a dangerous game of hide-and-seek, the forfeit of which was death. Daniel's enjoyment of the game is evident from the way he told the story of these experiences years later:

The Indians outwitted me one dark night, and I was unexpectedly as suddenly made a prisoner by them. The trick had been managed with great skill, for no sooner had I extinguished the fire of my camp, and laid me down to rest in full security, as I thought, than I felt myself seized by an indistinguishable number of hands, and was immediately pinioned, as if about to be led to the scaffold for execution. To have attempted to be refractory would have proved useless and dangerous to my life; and I suffered myself to be removed from my camp to theirs, a few miles distant, without uttering even a word of complaint. You are aware, I dare say, that to act in this manner was the best policy, as you understand that by so doing I proved to the Indians at once that I was born and bred as fearless of death as any of themselves.

When we reached the camp, great rejoicings were exhibited. Two squaws and a few pappooses appeared particularly delighted at the sight of me, and I was assured by very unequivocal gestures and words, that, on the morrow, the mortal enemy of the Redskins would cease to live. I never opened my lips, but was busy contriving some scheme which might enable me to give the rascals the slip before dawn. The women immediately fell a searching my hunting-shirt for whatever they might think valuable, and, fortunately for me, soon found my flask filled with Monongahela [strong whisky]. A terrific grin was exhibited on their murderous countenances, while my heart throbbed with joy at the anticipation of their intoxication. The crew immediately began to beat their bellies and sing, as they passed the bottle from mouth to mouth. How often did I wish the flask ten times its size, and filled with aqua fortis! I observed that the squaws drank more freely than the warriors, and again my spirits were about to be depressed, when the report of a gun was heard in the distance. The singing and drinking were both brought to a stand, and I saw, with inexpressible joy, the men walk off to some distance and talk to the squaws. I knew they were consulting about me, and I foresaw that in a few moments the warriors would go to discover the cause of the gun having been fired so near their camp. I expected the squaws would be left to guard me. Well, sir, it was just so. They returned; the men took up their guns and walked away. The squaws sat down again, and in less than five minutes had my bottle up to their dirty mouths, gurgling down their throats the remains of the whisky.

With what pleasure did I see them becoming more and more drunk, until the liquor took such hold of them that it was quite impossible for these women to be of any service. They tumbled down, rolled about, and began to snore; when I, having no other chance of freeing myself from the cords that fastened me, rolled over and over towards the fire, and, after a short time, burned them asunder. I rose on my feet, stretched my stiffened sinews, snatched up my rifle, and, for once in my life, spared that of Indians. I now recollect how desirous I once or twice felt to lay open the skulls of the wretches with my tomahawk; but, when I again thought of killing beings unprepared and unable to defend themselves, it looked like murder without need, and I gave up the idea.

But, sir, I felt determined to mark the spot, and, walking to a thrift ash sapling, I cut out of it three large chips, and ran off. I soon reached the river, soon crossed it, and threw myself deep into the canebrakes, imitating the tracks of an Indian with my feet, so that no chance might be left for those from whom I had escaped to overtake me.

It is now nearly twenty years since this happened, and more than five since I left the whites' settlements, which I might probably never have visited again had I not been called on as a witness in a lawsuit that was pending in Kentucky, and which I really believe would never have been settled, had I not come forward and established the beginning of a certain boundary line. This is the story, sir: Mr. —— moved from old Virginia into Kentucky, and having a large tract granted him in the new State, laid claim to a certain parcel of land adjoining Green River, and, as chance would have it, took for one of his corners the very ash tree on which I had made my mark, and finished his survey of some thousands of acres, beginning, as it is expressed in the deed, "at an ash marked by three distinct notches of the tomahawk of a white man."

The tree had grown much, and the bark had covered the marks; but, somehow or other, Mr. —— heard from some one all that I have already said to you, and thinking that I might remember the spot alluded to in the deed, but which was no longer discoverable, wrote for me to come and try to at least find the place of the tree. His letter mentioned that all of my expenses should be paid, and, not caring much about once more going back to Kentucky, I started and met Mr. ——. After some conversation, the affair with the Indians came to my recollection. I considered for a while, and began to think that after all, I could find the very spot, as well as the tree, if it was yet standing.

Mr. ——— and I mounted our horses, and off we went to the Green River bottoms. After some difficulties—for you must be aware, sir, that great changes have taken place in those woods—I found at last the spot where I had crossed the river, and, waiting for the moon to rise, made for the course in which I thought the ash tree grew. On approaching the place, I felt as if the Indians were there still, and as if I were still a prisoner among them. Mr. ——— and I camped near what I conceived the spot, and waited until the return of day.

At the rising of the sun, I was on foot, and after a good deal of musing, thought that an ash tree then in sight must be the very one on which I had made my mark. I felt as if there could be no doubt of it, and mentioned my thought to Mr. ———. "Well, Colonel Boone," said he, "if you think so, I hope it may prove true, but we must have some witnesses; do you stay hereabout, and I will go and bring some of the settlers whom I know." I agreed. Mr. ——— trotted off, and I, to pass the time, rambled out to see whether a deer was still living in the land. But ah! sir, what a wonderful difference thirty years make in a country! Why, at the time I was caught by the Indians, you would not have walked out in any direction for more than a mile without shooting a buck or a bear. There were then thousands of buffaloes on the hills of Kentucky; the land looked as if it never would become poor; and to hunt in those days was a pleasure indeed. But when I was left to myself on the banks of Green River, I dare say for the last time in my life, a few signs only of deer were to be seen, and, as to a deer itself, I saw none.

Mr. ——— returned, accompanied by three gentlemen. They looked upon me as I had been Washington himself, and walked to the ash tree, which I now called my own, as if in quest of a long-lost treasure. I took an axe from one of them, and cut a few chips off the bark. Still no signs were to be seen. So I cut again until I thought it was time to be cautious, and I scraped and worked away with my butcher-knife until I did come to where my tomahawk had left an impression in the wood. We now went regularly to work, and scraped at the tree with care until three hacks, as plain as any three notches ever were, could be seen. Mr. —— and the other gentlemen were astonished, and I must allow I was as much surprised as pleased myself. I made affidavit of this remarkable occurrence in presence of these gentlemen. Mr. —— gained the cause.

It was not long after the original incident which Boone describes so well that his younger brother returned with news and supplies of ammunition. They hunted and explored until the spring of 1771 and then Daniel returned to Carolina for his wife and children. He had decided to move them to Kentucky.

WHITE MAN ON THE WARPATH

Because of the manner in which his father had been killed and what he had seen of Indian cruelty to women and children, Lewis Wetzel hunted Indians as systematically as others hunted deer and buffalo. The redmen were his legitimate enemies and he thought nothing of setting out for a day's hunting of them. It was not unusual for Wetzel to track down a party of four Indians, shoot one dead from behind a tree and then, when the others set off in pursuit of him, elude them by superior woodsmanship.

Wetzel did not help Indian–white relations with this sort of action. The military leaders of the Kentucky area would have liked to take him into custody and indeed did so on several occasions. However, the pioneers loved him for these exploits; they not only admired him but protected him from the military.

One of Wetzel's most interesting exploits in the Kentucky area was when he rescued a young woman. A man who had been a childhood friend of Wetzel's family had come to Kentucky to settle, had fallen in love with a young girl there, and planned to marry her. He was on his way to her house when he ran across Wetzel and invited him to come with him. The two men walked through the woods, completely at ease, discussing their childhood. They came to the clearing in which stood the house of the young man's intended bride. The house was burned almost to the ground! The signs were evident and Wetzel could read them. A party of four warriors had come. They had taken away a single prisoner, the young girl the two men were coming to see.

Wetzel's young friend went wild with fury, fear, and excitement. Wetzel forced him to compose himself and agreed to take him on a search for his intended bride, with the understanding that the young man obey his orders unquestioningly.

They started off. Lewis decided to overtake the Indians and their captive. An ordinary woodsman would have found it difficult to find the Indians' trail, so carefully had they hidden it, but the faintest indication was significant to Wetzel, who followed after them with the unerring instinct of a bloodhound.

He soon became certain that the Indians were making for the Ohio River. After deciding this, Wetzel left the trail altogether and cut through the forest. He wanted to overtake them by a short route and cut off the party ahead.

When night came, Lewis and his young friend were still a good distance from the Ohio and their goal. They stopped for only a brief moment to swallow a few mouthfuls of food. Then they went on, Wetzel guiding them by the stars. Unfortunately the sky soon became overcast and they were forced to stop for the night. The next day, however, they started out early and as Wetzel had anticipated, crossed the trail of the Indians. The trail was a good few hours old, however, and their quarry was still ahead of them.

By afternoon they were almost upon the Ohio River and Lewis was certain they would catch up with the girl and her captors. It was not until nearly night, however, that they reached the banks of the Ohio and were able to see on the other side the camp site of those whom they sought. They swam the

Ohio and were soon watching the savages from a safe distance. Wetzel's companion was frantic once he observed his sweetheart but the older man restrained him from action. The young man had no cause to object, especially when Wetzel told him he had decided that daybreak was the hour at which they would attack.

At dawn the Indians were awake and preparing for their journey when Wetzel and his young friend fired simultaneously. Each brought down a target, which left only two Indians. They immediately fled, with Wetzel in pursuit, and the young man dashed into the Indian camp to free his sweetheart.

Wetzel was particularly famous for his ability to reload his gun on the run. Knowing that each gun had but one shot at a time, the Indians always underestimated his ability to kill. This time, he fired his gun at random, so as to draw out the fleeing savages. Supposing him to be defenseless, they came out of concealment with uplifted tomahawks. Wetzel had his gun reloaded by the time they appeared and immediately shot the nearest one through the head.

The surviving Indian knowing that Wetzel's gun was now truly empty, bounded at him. Wetzel dodged his pursuer from tree to tree. He ran here and there, avoiding the tomahawk the Indian was ever ready to hurl at him. It did not take long before his gun was reloaded. At this point he turned, faced the Indian, and killed him.

And so the lovers were reunited and lived happily ever after. Wetzel, by his physical agility and quick thinking and ability to use weapons of all kinds, continued his career of hate until he had repaid many times, and with interest, his father's death.

EPILOGUE

Daniel Boone died in 1820 at the age of eighty-six.
Lewis Wetzel died in 1808.
Both men were woodsmen in the true sense of the word, possessing skill in woodcraft and a deep feeling of idenity with

the forest. Both men contributed immeasurably to the development of America's frontier. Their fame inspired many who came after them, setting an example of courage and the adventurous spirit that was responsible for American expansion.

Of Sea-Going Snakes

People are always seeing things. Sometimes the things they see are there, and sometimes they are not. Sometimes some people can see things and some cannot even when they are there. And sometimes some can see things and some cannot when they are not there at all. Now I've seen things that other people haven't seen, and there have been other people who have seen things that I was not able to see. Anyway . . .

THE SPIRITS of two men are the true foundation of the American Navy. Both of them fought in the American Revolutionary War, both accomplished heroic deeds—yet, while the name of one of them, John Paul Jones, is known to all, the name of the other is very seldom heard. This second man fought wildly, impulsively, and with nerves of steel in the Revolutionary War; his planning and execution of the war with the Barbary pirates was a masterpiece of naval campaigning. His name was Edward Preble.

Not only is the name of Edward Preble comparatively unknown to the average American, but it is a fact that despite his naval accomplishments he was never rewarded with the status of admiral. The reason for this had nothing to do with his history as a fighting man but was the result of a record dating back to his first days at sea. You see, the scientists of the time had proved, at least to their own satisfaction, that there were no such things as sea serpents . . . and Edward Preble had reported in 1779 that he had seen one. It happened in this way:

At the beginning of the American Revolution, Congress commissioned privateers and thus made itself a navy. Young Edward Preble was one of the first to receive a commission

117

as midshipman and was assigned to duty with the Massachusetts Naval Service. In the year 1779, he was ordered to the United States privateer *Protector,* commanded by Captain Williams. While serving on the *Protector,* Preble saw the serpent.

On one of the bays of the Eastern coast the good ship *Protector* was lying at anchor waiting for supplies. It was a calm day, and there was very little excitement until the sailor at the helm screamed to the captain, "A monster is in the water!"

Captain Williams watched the apparition through his glasses and decided it was obviously one of the fabled sea serpents. The creature was motionless, its head out of the water; its body was at least 150 feet long.

The captain ordered young Midshipman Preble to man a boat and proceed to destroy the creature. Taking twelve armed men with him, Preble went over the side into a boat and pulled directly for the serpent. As he later described it, "The serpent was as thick as a barrel, as you could see from the serpentine loops that undulated out of the water. Its head was at least ten feet above the water."

There is something about a boatload of small humans pulling over the water toward a monster of this size that is not as brave as it is foolhardy. Nevertheless, Preble gave his men orders, and they were obeyed. We can only wonder at the emotions of the twelve sailors. Perhaps it was fortunate that this was a shy sea serpent. As the boat neared, the serpent turned its head toward the men for a minute, and then began to move slowly away from them. With the same foolhardiness, however, Preble soon had his men pulling with all their might. The self-possessed sea serpent merely glided away all the faster and finally disappeared, whether by submerging or by passing beyond the horizon we are not told.

After his discharge from the American Navy in 1783, Preble went into the Merchant Marine and was in command of the *Pickering* in 1798, when a quasi-war with France began. He then took command of theAmerican Navy's operations against the Barbary States.

It is a fact that Preble in his later years refused to talk about the incident of the sea serpent. Perhaps he was bitter about its effect on his naval career, perhaps he just did not care. At any rate, he knew he had seen something which the scientists of his day had declared did not exist.

The question arises as to whether or not he and the other men of the *Protector* did or did not see anything. It is undeniable that many sober men did see *something*. Was it a sea serpent? Are there sea serpents?

As a matter of fact, events point to the fact that though it is infrequently seen, there is an *American* sea serpent. Let us not talk about the sea serpents of other waters, nor sea serpents of antiquity, nor of the sea serpents reported by scientists very recently off Norway or in the Caribbean. No creature has yet been taken and examined that has not proved to belong to an already known category of sea creatures.

As for the existence of an American sea serpent, some very prominent men of learning, as well as fishermen and housewives, have seen it. In 1817, a sea serpent appeared off the coast of Gloucester, Massachusetts, where it was seen by many people. During the next year a sentry at Castle Island in Boston Harbor observed the sea serpent for about an hour before it disappeared. In August of 1819, it was again observed off the coast of Massachusetts, and this time it was seen by hundreds of people. It was described as being from sixty to eighty feet in length. It rose in the water with undulating movements and at times all of its body would disappear, except for its head. It moved rapidly, with a white foam under the head and a long wake. Thomas Perkins, founder of the Perkins Institute for the Blind in New England, said that the snake had a movement like the vertical movement of a caterpillar. Its color was dark brown.

The next and last-known appearance of this marine creature was in 1850, off the coast of the same New England area. Many saw the great snake undulating before their very eyes.

It is a strange thing that in every instance of the snake's appearance those who at first discussed with avidity what they had seen gradually stopped speaking about it, so unwilling was society to believe them. Edward Preble lies still unvindicated by the navy—but then, he has found out the truth by now.

FROM

A Wayfarer's Notebook:
Nineteenth Century

THE ABUNDANCE of food in America startled European visitors in the early nineteenth century as much as it does visitors today. In 1810, one John Melish, a visitor from England, described this scene with his landlady:

As I proposed to ride to New Philadelphia, 36 miles from Coshocton, and the road was altogether new to me, and often crossed the river, I was anxious to be gone as soon as possible, and urged the landlady to make all the haste she could. She said she would have the breakfast ready in a minute; but the first indication I saw of dispatch was a preparation to twist the necks of two chickens. I told her to stop, and she gave me a look of astonishment. "Have you any eggs?" said I. "Yes, plenty," replied she, still keeping in a stooping posture, with the chickens in her hand. "Well," said I, "just boil an egg, and let me have it, with a little bread and tea, and that will save you and I a great deal of trouble." She seemed quite embarrassed, and said she never could set down a breakfast to me like that. I assured her I would take nothing else. "Shall I fry some ham for you along with the eggs?" said she. "No," said I, "not a bit." "Well, will you take a little stewed pork?"

121

"No." . . . "Preserve me, what will you take then?"
"A little bread and tea, and an egg." *"Well, you're
the most extraordinary man that I ever saw; but I
can't set down a table that way." I saw that I was
only to lose time by contesting the matter farther; so
I allowed her to follow her own plan as to the cooking, assuring her that I would take mine as to eating.
She detained me about half an hour, and at last
placed upon the table a profusion of ham, eggs, frit-
ters, bread, butter, and some excellent tea. All the
time I was at breakfast, she kept pressing me to eat;
but I kept my own council, and touched none of the
dishes, except the bread, tea, and an egg. She af-
fected great surprise, and when I paid her the ordinary fare, a quarter of a dollar, she said it was hardly
worth anything. I mention the circumstance to show
the kind of hospitality of the landlady, and the good
living enjoyed by the* backwoods people.

❋

A TRAVELER, being exceedingly thirsty, stopped at a house by
the roadside and asked for a drink of milk. He emptied several
cups and asked for more. The woman of the house at length
brought out a large bowl filled with milk, and setting it down
on the table, remarked, "A person would think, sir, that you
had never been weaned."

❋

A PEDDLER asked an old lady if she could tell him of any road
that no peddler had ever traveled. "I know of but one," said
she, "and that is the road to Heaven."

❋

Two Boston divines disputing about the pronunciation of the word "either"—one saying it was *ee*-ther, the other *eye*-ther—agreed to refer it to the first person they met, who happened to be an Irishman. He confounded both by declaring, "It's nayther, for it's ayther."

*

ON MEN AND WOMEN
IN THE NEWSPAPERS: 1820

Who marries for love takes a wife; who marries for convenience takes a mistress; who marries from consideration takes a lady. You are loved by your wife, regarded by your mistress, tolerated by your lady. You have a wife for yourself, a mistress for your house and its friends, a lady for the world. Your wife will agree with you, your mistress will accommodate you, your lady will manage you. Your wife will take care of your household, your mistress of your house, your lady of appearances. If you are sick, your wife will nurse you, your mistress will visit you, your lady will inquire after your health. You take a walk with your wife, a ride with your mistress, and join parties with your lady. Your wife will share your grief, your mistress your money, and your lady your debts. If you are dead, your wife will shed tears, your mistress lament, and your lady wear mourning.

Marriage à la Mode

"Tom, you should take a wife." *"Nay, God forbid!"*
"I found you one last night." *"The deuce you did!"*
"Softly! Perhaps she'll please you." *"Oh, of course!"*
"Eighteen." *"Alarming!"* "Witty." *"Nay, that's worse!"*
"Discreet." *"All show!"* "Handsome." *"To lure the fellows."*
"High-born." *"Ay, haughty!"* "Tender-hearted." *"Jealous!"*

"Talents o'erflowing." "*Ay, enough to sluice me!*"
"And then, Tom, such a fortune!" "*Introduce me!*"

❋

THE PROBLEM of the Indians was a life-and-death matter to
the people on the ever-westward-pushing frontier. It was natural that a settler striving to wrest a livelihood for himself and
his family would have little patience for the rights of the redman. An interesting solution to the problem was that of William H. Crawford, Secretary of War to President Madison,
who recommended that the government encourage intermarriage between Indians and whites on the frontier.

Mr. Crawford's opponents made political capital out of this
and in Philadelphia there were published:

STRICTURES

Addressed to James Madison

on

The Celebrated Report

of

William H. Crawford,

Recommending

the

Intermarriage

of

Americans with the Indian Tribes.

Ascribed to Judge Cooper,

And originally published

By John Binns, in the Democratic Press

Philadelphia:

Printed by Jasper Harding.

1824

One of the documents included was a satirical letter, ostensibly written by one Tabitha Spinster to the Honourable Secretary of War, attempting to apply humor to a bad situation:

Maidenhead, New Jersey
May 1, 1816

To the Honourable the Secretary of War:
Sir:—Having seen your benevolent project for civilizing the Indians, by negotiating intermarriage with white people, I am encouraged to request you will take my case into your consideration. You must know, sir, that I am what is reproachfully styled an old maid, which, I assure you, is more my misfortune than my fault; for never poor damsel took greater pains to get married, than I have done, for the last fourteen years. I have regularly set my cap at everything in the shape of a man, that came into our village, and once thought I had entangled the parson of our parish, by means of certain pious conversations which took place between us, but discovered, to my utter mortification, some time afterwards, that he only came to our house to ogle a rich widow over the way.

My third attempt was upon the schoolmaster, a smooth, sleek, rosy-faced young fellow from Connecticut, who was somewhat of a scholar, a prig and a beau. He was a great favourite in the town, and the ladies always tittered a little when he came into church, to the great annoyance of the parson, who would not bear they should look at anybody but himself, I believe. I tried hard for the schoolmaster, and studied grammar on purpose to conjugate that charming verb "I love." We used to take moonlight walks along the mill pond, sit on a rock under a beautiful elm, and talk about the twelve signs, the crab, the twins, the virgin, and other monsters, and all that sort of thing. We were getting by little and little to the point, when one night I went with him to a Methodist meeting, when he was struck down, and afterwards went a-preaching among the back woods. I have since learned that he got to be a member of Congress afterwards.

But I should tire you, sir, and take up too much of your time, which belongs to the public and the Indians, if I were to detail all my attempts upon that impregnable fortress, the heart of man. I will, therefore, without further preface, being a woman of few words, come directly to the object of this letter. I would recommend, therefore, that all the old maids, whose case is considered desperate, be forthwith given in marriage to the Indians, who, though rather alarming sort of husbands, are certainly better than no husbands at all. For my part, though I have no great stomach for cooking dinner, and then waiting till my husband is satisfied before I partake of it; or for traversing the wilderness with a papoose at my back; still all circumstances considered, my situation cannot be much worse than it is, and I am willing to become an instrument in this benevolent plan of introducing the Indians to some degree of fellowship with the whites, and bringing them into subjection to the rules of civilized life. I learned to dance cotillons of a French dancing master, who sometimes made a summer campaign amongst us; I can stitch herring bone, spin street yarn, and skim cream, and in the management of that great instrument for reducing men to order, the tongue, I do flatter myself, sir, that I excel most women, married or single.

If, therefore, you could negotiate a match between me and some tall young Indian, I should take it as a particular favor. It would not become me to pick or choose, but I should prefer having a chief, with a good number of scalps for a necklace, and whose name had been mentioned in the world. Tecumseh, I am told, is dead, but Split Log is a good matrimonial name, and Little Turtle sounds very sentimentally. But I confess I should not like to be called Mrs. "Mad Dog," or Mrs. "Great Buffalo," or Mrs. "Wind that passes," or any of those names that make such a figure in our Indian treaties, with a great cross to them, as if they were Roman Catholics. However, beggars must not be choosers, and rather than not become an instrument in this great and original plan, I would consent to be called Mrs. Chefuskumclincumclacckmannicum, which in English, I am told, means Mrs. Devil, the Lord forgive me! Pray, sir, shall I hear from you soon.

I have the honour, etc., etc.
Tabitha Spinster

✿

AN ENGLISHMAN traveling in America asked an enthusiastic American lady why her country could not rest satisfied with the immense unoccupied territories it already possessed, but must ever be hankering after the lands of its neighbors. Her reply was, "Oh, the propensity is a very bad one, I admit; but we came honestly by it, for we inherited it from England."

✿

As WE know, among the people who rushed to California to find gold, many made their fortune in all the other popular ways—from the land, by selling food and materials, by going into many sorts of professions. However, some fortunes from the gold rush were made in the East. All kinds of things were sold to aid the California-bound gold seeker.

Here is a miscellany of advertisements taken from several Eastern newspapers in 1849. You could find duplicates of these in every city.

CALIFORNIA GOLD—*Instructions for collecting, testing, melting and assaying Gold, with a description of the process of distinguishing gold from worthless ores, for the use of persons going to California. Letter and cap paper, ink, inkstands, quills, wafers, sealing wax, gold and steel pens, traveling writing desks, chessmen, backgammon boards, playing cards, dominoes, money belts, envelopes, pocketbooks, pen-knives, portfolios, letter stamps, etc.* FRANCIS & LOUTREL, *Stationers, 77 Maiden Lane.*

CALIFORNIA—*Persons going to California will find at Agate's, 287 Broadway, a great variety of goods suitable for the above climate—shirts, plain and figured undershirts, drawers, money belts, body belts (an excellent article to prevent seasickness) and a variety of articles too numerous to mention.*

CALIFORNIANS—*The change you will meet in climate and diet produces violent dysentery, witness every letter from the mines and Isthmus. A pleasant and warranted cure is sold at 117 Maiden Lane, upstairs.*

TO CALIFORNIA—*A gentleman is about forming a company of 50 to 75 persons to proceed to Vera Cruz and thence through by land to San Francisco. A competent and experienced person will guide and take charge of the expedition. None but persons who can command $300 to $500 and produce unexceptionable references as to character for temperance need apply, as the object of the party is to form a* *responsible company for self preservation. Address box 880 with real name, reference and profession, which will receive immediate attention.*

Here are some from the *Boston Evening Traveller* of January 31, 1849:

CALIFORNIA GOODS—*G. C. Holman 15 & 17 Kilby Street, invites attention to his large assortment of Fancy and Staple Goods, adapted to the California and Pacific Trade, on which Shippers and Adventurers will be sure to realize handsome profits. The assortment embraces beads, jewelry, mirrors, soap, colognes, brushes, combs, cutlery, purses, cigar cases, tobacco and snuff boxes, Indian bells, etc.*

CALIFORNIA—*Persons going to California should be sure and take some of the celebrated "Antique Chinese Hair Oil," that they may possess a beautiful head of Hair on their return. For sale at wholesale and retail at the Price, 37½ cents per bottle.*

CHINA TEA STORE
198 Washington Street

Gabriel, Blow Your Horn!

This story of one of the adventures of the Reverend Lorenzo Dow is to me rich in humor and flavor. It is told here with respect for the spirited dedication of the worthy preacher, and also for his ready wit.

ONE OF the most interesting characters of the Chesapeake Bay area at the turn of the nineteenth century was the Reverend Lorenzo Dow, who was known along the Pocomoke River as the "Travelin' Preacher." His fervor and dramatic approach converted thousands of the river people from the ways of the Devil to the ways of God.

To survive the long, hard workdays and scarcity of comforts—and sometimes necessities—the folks who lived and fished along Maryland's Eastern Shore had to have a sense of humor. And this man of religion was no exception.

One spring day in 1807, Reverend Dow was scheduled to address some two thousand persons in the town of Newton on the Pocomoke. Since the church itself was too small for the expected crowd and since the day was a warm and beautiful one, the congregation was to assemble outside. A little ahead of time, the preacher arrived in the churchyard.

Happy to be alone for a few minutes to collect his thoughts, Dow was suddenly startled to hear a small voice say, "Howdy, Brother Dow."

He could see no one.

The voice repeated, "Brother Dow. Howdy."

The good Reverend looked about to no avail. From where came this heavenly voice?

"Up here, Brother Dow."

He looked up. Perched in the big elm tree was a little colored boy named Gabriel. He was all teeth and squirms, giggling with delight at having foolishness with the great preacher.

Dow noticed that little Gabriel clutched his most precious possession, an old tin horn. "Gabriel" and "horn"! Reverend Dow strode purposefully to the base of the tree.

"Gabriel," he said in his most persuasive voice, "would you like to have a dollar?"

"A dollar?" Gabriel nearly fell out of the tree.

"My boy, you may have half of that dollar now and one half when the meeting is over . . . if . . . if you do *exactly* what I tell you to do."

Gabriel did not require argument; he would have done anything.

"You just sit where you are," explained Reverend Dow. "Do not make a sound while I'm preaching. And when I say 'Blow, Gabriel'—*then* you blow your horn!"

Now the subject of the Reverend Mr. Dow's preachment that day was "The Resurrection and The Day of Judgment." He spoke as one inspired. His audience hung on every word, carried along by his fervor.

Working up to the climax, Reverend Dow told of the Angel Gabriel standing with one foot on the Sea and one on the Land, his long silver trumpet in his hand. . . .

"Blow, Gabriel!" Mr. Dow shouted suddenly.

And Gabriel blew his horn!

And the congregation fell on the ground crying for mercy, shouting salvation. The horses staked nearby were frightened and added to the uproar by squealing and stamping.

Up in the tree, little Gabriel was delighted. So he blew his horn again.

Gabriel's mother looked up and shouted, "You come down here, Gabriel!" And the shamed sinners looked up and slowly rose to their knees.

They looked menacingly at their spiritual leader. But as always, he was equal to the situation.

"If a little boy can strike such terror into your hearts," he shouted, "What will you do when the great day really comes?"

"Amen," cried the congregation. "Amen!"

The Privateer Turned Patriot

I have watched many people from foreign countries confronted with, and baffled by, the problem of becoming an American. I have seen them sever the emotional tie with their fatherland and embrace their new home. This moment, it seems, comes as a rebirth, and it is this rebirth that has made America great. But I have seen them remain baffled, unto the second generation, by not being able to think like Americans—and above all by not being able to understand how the American thinks. Men who have fought for their new country find it easier to understand these things. Or men who love a place as Jean Lafitte loved New Orleans.

THERE WAS an over-sized four-poster bed in the big room. The form lying beneath the sheets sighed deeply, then suddenly sat up to reveal bare bronzed shoulders, a black matted chest, a rakishly awry black mustache, and a wildly snarled head of black hair.

"Jacqueline!" this person roared. "Jacqueline!"

A shuffling movement from the other side of the door showed that, as always, Jacqueline was not far off. In a moment the door opened and she padded in, her *café-au-lait* face wreathed in a smile so wide it showed her back teeth.

"*Bon matin*, M'sieu Lafitte. You slept well?"

She was carrying a small bedside table and, putting it down, she poured a cup of steaming chocolate, which she offered to her reclining master, along with a crisp, warm *croissant*.

After pulling back the curtains, she backed out of the room, smiling and bobbing her head. While the person in the bed twisted his mustache and felt all was right with the world, the retreating Negress thought what an absurd, small figure he was sleeping in that big bed.

This bed and many other furnishings of the house were prizes from a Spanish sailing ship looted on its way home to Barcelona from Cartagena. The bed was shaped like a giant gondola. Capering cupids clambered up the four posts. The canopy was of golden brocade, embellished with the crest of an aristocratic Spanish family. On the headboard two fat cherubs smiled lovingly down, in mahogany relief, on the pillows below. Let it be said the pillows were sheathed in the finest silk. The sheets, too, were of silk, and the single coverlet was of crimson, embroidered all over with winged figures, delicate flowers, and bows and arrows.

It was the Spanish crest that particularly delighted the heart of the man who was lying in the bed. To beat the Spanish satisfied a hate he had admitted to but never explained. Although he never discussed his life as it was before his arrival in New Orleans in 1804, a casual remark or dropped reference indicated to his lieutenants that he came from the border region of France and Spain, perhaps even from the Basque country, and had suffered mightily at the hands of the Spanish.

This morning Lafitte rose from the bed, walked to the window, and looked out on the early morning sunlight. His house was on an elevation commanding the entire island of Grand Terre and offered a fine view of the Gulf of Mexico. Between the house and the beach he could see his warehouses filled with contraband merchandise waiting to be sold. There, too, were the barracoons, where African slaves, stolen from slave ships, waiting in moaning dread for they knew not what fate.

It was 1814 and the slave trading and smuggling of Lafitte and his men were important to Louisiana's cotton-and-sugar economy. Large plantations had to be worked by the cheapest labor, which meant slaves. Also, the highly civilized citizenry of New Orleans, with its elegant women and elegant men, had to have the silks and satins and wines and furnishings of Europe. Jean Lafitte, his half brother, Pierre, and his many associates, particularly René Beluche and Dominique You, were sought after by New Orleans merchants and amiably ignored by the law enforcers whom they paid off.

As the tall, well-built buccaneer was dressing, he heard a new step in the next room. It was Dominique You, who called out agitatedly, "Jean!" He knocked and came in.

Dominique was the idealized picture of a pirate. Short, broad-shouldered, with fierce eyes, he had a vicious white scar from temple to chin which contributed greatly to the natural savagery of his face. Born in Port-au-Prince, he had been an adventurer and sea rover from boyhood. Despite his appearance, Dominique was good-natured and loved practical jokes. He was exceptionally brave.

"Jean," he said, breathless from running, "Jean, the British are in the Gulf! The lookout saw two, maybe three, men-of-war on the horizon. He thinks one of them has lowered a boat. The sun's reflection on the water makes it difficult to see. Soon we shall know if it is so and if we are to have callers."

Jacqueline knocked and entered with Lafitte's freshly laundered shirt, with its starched jabot and gracefully flounced cuffs. This she put carefully on the bed. Then she left to return a moment later with his washing and shaving materials: a jug of hot water, a porcelain basin, scented French soap, and a straight-edged razor. She put the case on the washstand under the decorated mirror and left.

"Give me five minutes to dress myself," Jean requested Dominique. "Then we go together to the lookout. If the British are sending a boat I do not want to look like a Cajun from the woods. Lafitte must look his part. The gentleman rover. The king of the smugglers, yes?"

Deftly, quickly, Lafitte shaved chin and jowls, trimmed his mustache, flattened his rowdy hair with the latest French pomade. Then he dressed carefully in soft doeskin trousers and the white starched silk shirt. He regarded his reflection in the mirror, saluted his handsome face with an imperious nod,

139

and then beckoned Dominique to follow him. They went through the sitting room, out onto the veranda, down the steps, and down the path leading to the lookout station.

Grand Terre, with its sister island, Grand Isle, are two slender islands eight miles long and a mile wide which form the Baratarian Archipelago. They separate Barataria Bay from the Gulf of Mexico. The islands are about a hundred miles south of New Orleans, at that time a two-day journey through impenetrable bayous, swamps, and marshes.

Standing, telescope in hand, at the Gulf side of the lookout station, Lafitte could barely make out in the sunlight the outlines of a long boat rowing toward them. As they watched, the boat grew clearer and larger, until they could make out the uniforms of British tars straining at the oars and a British officer sitting upright and correct midships.

Lafitte and his lookout went down to the landing dock. When the boat was about twenty feet away, the helmsman shouted, "Landing party of His Majesty's Fleet! On personal business to Jean Lafitte." The lookout had his rifle in firing position. Lafitte pushed the gun down. He called back to the boat, "I am Lafitte. Land in peace."

The boat scraped to a stop on the sand, and the officer stepped out.

"M'sieu Lafitte? I am Captain Lockyer, representative of Lieutenant Colonel Edward Nicholls, with an important document for your personal perusal, sir. It is indeed an honor and a fortunate coincidence that the great Jean Lafitte should be on hand to personally welcome us to Barataria."

"I am at your service, sir," rejoined Lafitte with his most disarming smile, bowing. "I must insist, before we burden ourselves with business, that we repair to my poor dwelling so that you may refresh yourself after so long a sea voyage."

Lafitte led the way along the paths to his home, volubly discussing the sea, the day, the fortunes of Napoleon, the latest news from abroad, punctuating his remarks with broad gestures and deep rumbling chuckles. Lockyer answered courteously, but his attention was taken with the cosy palmetto-thatched cottages that nestled snugly in thickets of shrub and oleander, which was where the Baratarians lived. When they came clear of the thicket, he could not help but exclaim in amazement at the sight of Lafitte's house. This was a rambling, one-story dwelling, constructed of brick and coated on the outside with a mixture of pulverized oyster shell and plaster, a mixture of Lafitte's own invention. Surrounded by trees and flowers, it stood above all else on the island. There were iron bars on the many large windows and a wide veranda on which Lafitte spent the few leisure hours he allowed himself. A bright red hammock testified to his mode of relaxation.

With the exception of the bed, described earlier, and undoubtedly used by Lafitte as a caprice, the pirate was a man of excellent good taste and fastidious judgment. Lockyer (who did not see the bed) reported later that the furnishing of Lafitte's home was simple, utilitarian, and at the same time very elegant. Exquisite glassware served the best wines of France, gleaming silver was placed on the hand-woven linen on his table. Magnificent paintings and thick Oriental carpets gave each room a palatial grandeur.

Lafitte ushered Lockyer into a room of great comfort, where he worked, relaxed, entertained friends and, as on this day in 1814, September the third, listened to propositions and made deals. "My house is yours," he said, ushering the captain inside.

He turned to his guest, "The day is growing hot. May I suggest some lunch and then our traditional siesta? We can talk in the cool of the afternoon." Before Lockyer could say that he wanted to talk immediately, Lafitte was helping him out of his jacket and saying, "Do not worry about your men. They will be provided for. In the meantime, I must do an errand, but I will return to lunch with you." Lafitte went off. Outside the door he said to Jacqueline, "We'll let the beefeater fidget a while. Give him wine."

All through luncheon, Lafitte kept the conversation to trivialities. He refused to talk about the war between the United States and England or any other serious subject. By the meal's end, he was yawning copiously and openly. "I always sleep at midday during hot weather, Captain," he said. "May I suggest you revive yourself as well." There was little Lockyer could do but comply.

When Lockyer awoke in the late afternoon, refreshed and impatient to fulfill his mission, Lafitte was nowhere in sight. He found Jacqueline but she lapsed into Creole patois and professed to understand not one word of his English. There was nothing he could do but sit on the wide veranda and wait. Evening shadows lengthened but still no Lafitte. From inside the house Lockyer could hear a feverish activity of dishes and pots. He could only assume that he would be forced to stay to dinner and was certain it would be a good one. Loud voices interrupted the reverie into which he had fallen. Up the steps came Lafitte with his two trusted lieutenants, Dominique You and René Beluche. He introduced his English guest to his lieutenants, he apologized for being late. "We sip an *apéritif* outside here, no? Then I promise you Jacqueline has prepared for you one of her most wonderful dinners. We have dinner in your honor."

A wonderful dinner it was, served on Sèvres china, on Spanish damask. There were hors d'oeuvres of every description, made of Gulf shrimp and tiny mollusks and vegetables and herbs in vinaigrette sauce. These were followed by a crab gumbo that has since made New Orleans famous. Next came a steaming platter of roast wild turkey, stuffed with pecans and raisins, followed by a succulent red fish cooked in white wine. A rare selection of French and Italian cheeses and finally . . . coffee, Courvoisier, and a big Havana cigar.

"The French devil, he's playing with me," Lockyer thought to himself. He despaired of bringing the conversation around to his purpose when Lafitte suddenly spoke up: "Now, my good Captain, what message do you bring me from Colonel Nicholls?"

Lockyer cleared his throat, glanced inquiringly at You and Beluche.

"Speak in front of them freely," said Lafitte. "They are my trusted friends."

"Colonel Nicholls has asked me to hand you this letter personally."

Lafitte's face was serious as he read and then turned to his men. "Colonel Nicholls offers me thirty thousand pounds, captaincy of my own ship, and berths for every Baratarian who will join me. It will mean fighting against the Americans for the seizure of Louisiana by the British."

His two lieutenants looked at him in silence. "That is a lot of money," Lafitte seemed to be arguing. "A very good offer."

Lockyer felt that it was time for him to present the arguments as he knew them. "You are not a backwoodsman or a farmer; you are a gentleman, an aristocrat. This rough democracy is not for you. This United States is not your country. Is not your brother Pierre rotting in Cabildo Prison? Has not Governor Claiborne offered five hundred dollars for your apprehension? We of His Majesty's Navy understand a man like you. His Majesty's Navy will give you honor, reward, a proud ship of your own, and an assured high office in the British Government of Louisiana."

When Lafitte did not answer, Lockyer rose from his seat. "It grows late and I must be aboard. What shall I tell Colonel Nicholls, M'sieu Lafitte?"

Lafitte rose courteously. "Thank Colonel Nicholls for his most generous offer and tell him I must have two weeks to decide. He shall have his answer before September the eighteenth, no later."

Lockyer bowed, and farewells were exchanged. You accompanied him to the waiting British boat.

As soon as the Britisher was gone, Lafitte paced the terrace excitedly. No longer affable or delaying, he spoke with curt authority. "Beluche, we start for New Orleans tonight. We Louisianans have been American eleven years, and I like it.

I offer our services to Governor Claiborne. The condition is that he frees Pierre and grants us oblivion for past offenses. First we go to New Orleans and we confer with Edward Livingston. He and Grimes will deliver my offer to the governor. No, no, Beluche—I can see you are objecting. It is because you do not understand. Governor Claiborne hates me, yes, but we have one important thing in common. To us both, New Orleans is beautiful and must not be destroyed by British guns."

"Jacqueline!" he called. "Prepare food for two. We go up the bayous to New Orleans. Be sure to put in some of that turkey! *C'était magnifique!*" He turned to his lieutenants, "Prepare for the journey, René. Return in an hour. I must write the letter to Claiborne and change."

Between Barataria Bay and New Orleans lies a great semiliquid wilderness, through which linking bayous twist and turn for over one hundred miles. It is a maze of streams and swamps, generously strewn with oak-topped mounds ideal for hiding out. It is a confusion of lakes, so interwoven that a man could make a hundred round trips to New Orleans and never follow the same route twice. It is a land of brilliant blooms, stormy shores, calm inlets, somber Spanish moss, gay oleander and stunted oak, leaning away from the salt spray of the sea. It is a strange contrast of brash color and sinister dankness that is extremely beautiful.

Waiting for Lafitte was a *pirogue,* the French name given canoes of the lower Mississippi regions. The pirogue originated with the Indians, who burned out the trunks of cottonwoods and shaped the ends. It was improved on by the French, who felled fifty-foot cypresses that could carry twenty men or several tons of freight. Pirogues were the only sensible way to travel the bayous, since there were passages that were only inches deep. The two men stepped into their boat and paddled off into the night.

The moon was full, which made the mist over Bayou St.

Denis reflect eerily as the two men paddled through the water. From time to time they could see lazy alligators that moved slowly away as they approached. Here and there, a bull alligator did not move but rolled up one eyelid to look at the interlopers, then shut it again. Water moccasins slithered and wriggled away through the water. On the shore gray-blue herons and snowy egrets were sleeping. More seen than heard were the muskrats and even the occasional black bear. Here and there, startled deer moved away. Sticking up in the water were patches of land covered with live oaks, Indian mounds, and ancient refuse heaps of a bygone civilization. The men settled down to paddling in four-hour shifts as the night wore on, one paddling effortlessly while the other slept. There was no need to speak, and they were sure of their direction.

It was late in the afternoon of the second day when they reached a landing halfway between New Orleans and Chalmette, just one mile south of the New Orleans city gate. They beached the pirogue and walked toward the city.

New Orleans at this time was built like a medieval town. Situated on a bend of the Mississippi, it was protected on the land side by a moat forty feet wide and seven feet deep. There were four gates to the city, and these were closed at night and guarded. Inside, the buildings were built on French or Spanish styles or a mixture of both. The streets were crude and plentiful, a veritable marshland of mud and filth so bad that ladies of fashion dared not step into them for fear of ruining shoes and fine clothes. Rude carts with wheels and axles of solid wood creaked through the streets, a holdover from the Spanish governors, who had required them by law since squeaking discouraged smuggling. The population of the city at this time was about twenty-five thousand, made up of old Creole and Spanish families, Eastern whites, Negro freedmen and slaves, and mixtures of these.

At the corner of Chartres and St. Louis Streets was *La Bourse de Masperos* (a coffeehouse which still stands today

145

as Maspero's Exchange Coffee House). It was here that Lafitte and Beluche stopped for refreshment after their journey.

A small Negro boy was sent to fetch Edward Livingston and John Randolph Grimes, legal counsel and close friends of the Lafittes. Grimes could not be found but Livingston arrived just as the first effects of their absinthe began to mellow the two tired men. Livingston was fifty years old, extremely rich, and very conservative. Among his other contributions to Louisiana, he had prepared the provisional code of judicial procedure used for years in Louisiana. He had been a United States congressman from 1795 to 1801, district attorney of New York under Jefferson, and mayor of New York City. He had lived in New Orleans since its early years as a part of the United States.

When Pierre Lafitte had been arrested the previous year and thrown into the Cabildo jail, Jean had approached Grimes and Livingston and asked them to be his counsel and save Pierre for the sum of twenty thousand dollars. After talking with Lafitte, Livingston accepted the offer, even though, as he said, he did not need the money. Livingston had long been a personal friend and aide to Governor Claiborne, despite his defense of Pierre Lafitte, and was well thought of by the governor and Louisiana society.

But in spite of Livingston's efforts, Pierre Lafitte was still in chains. Jean's first question was to ask news of his brother.

The answer was not encouraging. "It is the same affair. We have tried every legal weapon at our disposal . . . and you know I know them all, including the plea of ill health. It is no avail. But what are you doing in New Orleans, Jean? There is a price on your head!"

"I am here with a letter I would like you to deliver to Governor Claiborne. Three days ago His Majesty's Government offered me thirty thousand pounds and a ship of my own if I joined them in the siege of New Orleans. I requested two weeks before answering. As you know, Mr. Livingston, New

Orleans is my home and my most beautiful city. I cannot see it destroyed. Beyond that, as a Frenchman, I cannot let those accursed British call on me for help."

"Don't you have any feeling as an American?" Livingston asked, quirking an eyebrow.

"Well," Lafitte replied, "the Americans have jailed Pierre, so at this time they are my enemies. But what my letter offers to their government is the services and equipment of all the Baratarians, with me to lead them. But only if—*if*, mind you— they will free Pierre and grant us oblivion for past offenses. The British have twelve thousand men, Mr. Livingston. Together, Claiborne and I can defend New Orleans. Without my help, the city is doomed."

Livingston stared at the man before him and accepted the letter. "The letter will be delivered. Now spend the night quietly and go back to Grand Terre. I will send you his decision in a few days. I must insist that you leave immediately."

Lafitte returned and waited in his house for four days, five days, seven days, eight days. There was no word from Livingston, and Lafitte became frantic with uncertainty. On the eighth day he sent another letter by courier. The courier returned four days later with a message from Livingston. Claiborne and his counsel had agreed that the notes were forged and had refused to take them seriously. Claiborne privately confided to Livingston that it would jeopardize his position to take Lafitte as an ally after years of publicly condemning his activities. Livingston warned that rumor was rife that Claiborne was planning to send an American gunboat to destroy the Baratarian settlement and Grand Terre.

Scarcely had Lafitte crumpled Livingston's message in his outraged fist when an excited runner informed him that two American gunboats were approaching the island. This could mean only one thing. Claiborne had actually decided to destroy the settlement. Beluche and You appeared, ready to fight. "We have supplies and men enough to stand them off for a month!" Beluche exulted.

147

Lafitte stared coldly at them. "We shall not fight Americans," he announced. "When a father strikes a child, it is no excuse for the child to turn on his father. Let us leave Grand Terre together and live in the marshes. If we fight against them now, win or lose, we will not be able to walk again in the streets of New Orleans."

The American gunboats had already started to fire as Lafitte and most of the Baratarians fled the islands in hastily loaded pirogues. Lafitte did not look back at the home which he knew he would never see again and at the island stronghold that had taken ten years of his life to build. Shouting, *"Bonne chance!"* to his fellow refugees, he called to them that their rendezvous would be the temple on Lake Salvador. Paddling furiously, the boats separated into the many bayous.

The few Baratarians who had preferred fight to flight put up a strong defense which lasted for four days. After which time, Master Commandant Patterson of the navy landed on Grand Terre and burned all the buildings, including Lafitte's home. He seized 500 thousand dollars worth of merchandise and equipment. He also captured Dominique You, who had stayed behind to fight.

Arriving at the temple rendezvous in Lake Salvador, Lafitte was greeted at the dock by a robust figure with large dark eyes and burnished light brown hair. He was unable to believe his eyes. "Pierre!" he yelled. "Pierre, you escaped!"

The brothers hugged and kissed each other on both cheeks, too moved to say very much. Pierre finally told his brother, "If you had but left Grand Terre one hour later, I could have traveled up the bayous with you. Livingston bribed a turnkey to let me escape, and I was on my way across Barataria Bay when I heard shooting. Then I met a pirogue bulging with men. They told me the rendezvous was here . . . and so *here* I am."

"We will not linger here," Jean Lafitte told his brother. "I have sent word to Livingston that we will encamp at Lac des

Allemands. I have told him we would be ready to fight the British whenever he can make Claiborne call us."

Claiborne, in the meantime, was sorely worried over the apathy of New Orleans in the face of imminent attack. Chill October rain fell in the muddy streets. More and more British vessels were reported in the Gulf. The Louisiana militia trained desultorily and by any estimate was greatly outnumbered by the enemy.

Lafitte and his men, finding Lac des Allemands damp and uncomfortable, moved in a body across the Cajun country to Last Island, two hundred miles west of Grand Terre in the Gulf of Mexico. Livingston was active on their behalf. On October 24 he wrote the story of their offer and its rejection, of the destruction of their home, directly to President Madison. He recommended a general pardon for the privateers, five hundred men who would be invaluable to the defense of New Orleans. More pertinently, he was able a week later to convince Claiborne of Lafitte's sincerity. Claiborne then also wrote to Washington, explaining that he needed the Baratarians' aid and asking the Attorney General to pardon them.

November passed in record suspense for New Orleans. There was no action from Washington and no action from the British, who seemed to be merely contemplating the city from afar. Lafitte's group on Last Island were housed in palmetto shelters, waiting with rigged boats for official acceptance.

It was on December 2 that a newcomer entered the scene. A jaundiced, emaciated, gaunt wreck of a man rode on horseback into New Orleans, slid exhausted from his horse, greeted Governor Claiborne with scant courtesy, and demanded an immediate review of the city's defenses. His eyes were black, burning, restless; ill with fever, his Spanish cloak caked with dried mud, General Andrew Jackson had ridden without stop across the country from Mobile, Alabama, accompanied by only a half-dozen officers.

The general staggered with illness but rigidly forced himself to do what was necessary. The condition of the city did not cheer him: there was Patterson's tiny navy of five gunboats and the *Carolina* and the *Louisiana;* Ross's seven hundred regulars, one thousand militia; a shortage of guns, ammunition, and flints. The British had twelve thousand hand-picked regulars fresh from their victory over Napoleon. It was a dismal prospect.

That evening at Maspero's where the general sat relaxing, he was approached by his old acquaintance, Edward Livingston, as dapper, astute, and charming as always. "General Jackson, I feel fortunate that the governor has appointed me to be your military secretary during your stay in our city. I hope I will prove of some small assistance in acquainting you with whatever local information will be of help."

The general looked at Livingston and motioned him to sit down. "Mr. Livingston, I am honored to have your services. The indifference of the city apalls me. Your militia trains as if it were doing us a favor. Don't the people of New Orleans realize that if the British attack, the city is doomed! We must have more ammunition, we must have more men, and we must have more spirit."

"There's Lafitte," Livingston suggested softly.

"A pirate? A murderer? A smuggler? Never!"

"He has refused an offer of the British Navy to fight against New Orleans. They offered him thirty thousand pounds. He loves New Orleans, General Jackson, and he is brave. Also, he is a fighter. He wants to help save New Orleans. He is even now waiting on Last Island in the Gulf with five hundred fighting men and great quantities of ammunition. All he needs is a word from you."

Jackson pondered for only a few minutes. "I will see Lafitte. Send for him."

Livingston smiled, "I sent for him, General Jackson, as soon as I knew you were in the city."

Three days later Jean Lafitte appeared at Maspero's in his

most elegant clothes. He climbed to the second floor with his dress sword clanking at his side and announced himself at the door of General Jackson's headquarters. Livingston was there waiting; he clasped his hand in greeting and himself knocked on the general's door. When a rasping voice bade the visitors enter, Livingston introduced Lafitte and immediately withdrew.

The general was not one to mince words. "Jean Lafitte, I have been used to calling your men pirates, robbers and banditti. Before we begin our talk, I want you to know I have not changed my mind. Livingston tells me you offer your men and munitions in the defense of New Orleans. You defend not only New Orleans but the United States. Does that mean anything to you?"

Lafitte bowed gravely, "I arrived in Louisiana a fugitive from France at almost the moment the United States made the Louisiana Purchase. I will protect this land to the best of my ability. If you wish it, my men and I and a full warehouse of flint and ammunition are at your service."

He and Jackson spoke and planned for about a half an hour before Lafitte saluted and left the room. On his way out, one of Jackson's officers asked, "Are you the Frenchman Lafitte?"

It is a matter of record that Lefitte drew himself up and answered, "*Mais non, m'sieu, je suis l'américain* Lafitte!"

On December 14, the British discovered that the American Navy, such as it was, lay in Lake Borgne, some thirty miles west of New Orleans. The five American gunboats, under the command of Lieutenant Thomas Jones, were on that day totally disabled by British fire, and the only notation on the credit side of the ledger was that the attack delayed the British march on New Orleans and gave Old Hickory precious days of extra time. It was not till ten days later that an American patrol galloping wildly into New Orleans, announced that a vanguard of the British Army had encamped at the Villeré plantation, only nine miles down the Mississippi.

The pain-racked Jackson reviewed his command of about two thousand men, half of whom had never seen action. Within a matter of hours Jackson personally led an attack on the Villeré plantation and doubtless saved New Orleans. General Pakenham's British grenadiers were so amazed at the savagery of these ragged, ill-formed ranks that they assumed there must be thousands of mad Americans eager for British blood. They fled.

Once again, Old Hickory had postponed the inevitable siege of the city. The attack on New Orleans began in earnest on January 8. Lafitte, Beluche, and You reported to Jackson's headquarters.

"Beluche . . . You . . ." Jackson ordered crisply, "I hereby make you captains of artillery. By reputation you are the best cannoneers in these parts. Now you can prove it. As for you, Lafitte,"—the general turned and faced him squarely—"I need your help in a way which will not reflect on your personal courage. But it may mark you as a coward to those ignorant of the facts. Well?"

It was a surprisingly humble Lafitte who waited for his orders and did not question them. "I am your servant, General," he replied.

"The British will attack over land, of this I am almost certain. Yet I cannot risk the possibility of a secret march from the sea. You must make a defense at Lake Salvador. You are the one man who can lead, who knows the bayous and marshes south of the city, and you can keep the redcoats at bay if they come that way."

"All the principal bayous terminate at Lake Salvador. A water moccasin could not slither past the men I take with me." Lafitte bowed and went on his mission.

As daylight brightened, the British advanced in mass formation against the New Orleans forces, now numbering over five thousand men with the arrival of a division from Kentucky. They fired from behind a rude earthwork parapet five feet high and twenty feet thick. While the battle raged, the ladies of New Orleans, whether quadroon or of fine family, huddled together in frightened groups with daggers in their belts. They had been told what would happen if the town fell and were determined to kill themselves at sight of the redcoats.

The morning wore on. Beluche and You directed their cannon with riotous shouts and increasing excitement. Tennessee and Kentucky riflemen, spitting chewing tobacco, quietly and calmly picked off the brilliant red targets one at a time like clay pigeons in a gallery. Lafitte and his men waited impatiently for action on Lake Salvador.

By eleven in the morning, it was obvious that there would be no attack from the sea, and Jackson sent word for Lafitte to move his men to Chalmette, across the Mississippi, and strengthen the flank of the defenders. Obediently Lafitte ordered a quick march and arrived at noon.

Before the afternoon had ended, the fighting was over. The British sailed away with two thousand casualties, including the death of General Pakenham.

That night when Lafitte walked through the wildly celebrating streets, light-headed, exultant over the victory, cries of *"Vive Lafitte!"* and "Long live the Baratarians!" greeted him.

At Jackson's headquarters Lafitte waited his turn for an audience with the general. Jackson rose to greet him for the first time and shook his hand. "You have contributed to our victory, Lafitte. This was the most decisive battle of the war."

On January 21 Jackson issued a proclamation to the city, commending Jean and Pierre Lafitte, Dominique You, René Beluche, and all the Baratarians. He pardoned them at the same time for all their previous crimes.

Two days later there was a public thanksgiving in New Orleans at the Place D'Armes, later named Jackson Square. At the stroke of noon Old Hickory entered the river gate with his staff and proceeded through the Arc de Triomphe. A victory ball was held that night, attended by not only all New Orleans society but by Jean Lafitte and his lieutenants.

As the ball drew to a close, Jackson stopped to exchange remarks with Governor Claiborne and Lafitte, who were standing together. "Governor Claiborne. Lafitte. It does my heart good to see you in harmony in the midst of this celebration." He looked at the dancing throng, "I believe that we three who stand here together and deprive the ladies of our accomplishments are possibly the most sought-after gentlemen here."

A Trail of Tall Tales

Put a bunch of males together—be they roosters, dogs, or men—and in a remarkably short time the contest for superiority is on. Set a bunch of men down in a frontier town, with only an occasional woman to accentuate the struggle, and you will soon find the strongest man imposing his personal law: lawlessness. Place them on keelboats on a river—and a Mike Fink emerges to take on all comers with no holds barred.

IN 1820, Cairo, Illinois, at the junction of the Ohio and Mississippi Rivers, had a few buildings, a few log cabins and a few warehouses for flatboat stores. Mr. Montgomery, owner of a Cairo warehouse, had lost two flatboats in the last six weeks on the swollen waters of the Mississippi. What is more, it was proving very expensive to get new flatboats and a new crew every time it was necessary to take a cargo down the river. Thinking the situation over, he decided he could make a better profit if he could bring upriver sugar, cotton, and many of the European goods that flooded into New Orleans. The answer was simple. He had to have a boat that could go downstream with a good-sized cargo and be brought up by using the principle of the lever on the river bottom.

He was not the first man to face this problem, nor the first to decide that a keelboat was the answer. He built himself the first keelboat in what soon became a line of about fifteen such botas. He built his boat upon a keel, with a framework of ribs to which planking was attached. The loaded keelboat, he figured, would not draw more than two feet of water. The keel could be so constructed that it would absorb the impact of rocks an dother submerged objects.

When the boat was finished, Mr. Montgomery set about getting the man with the reputation for handling his crews most successfully and getting cargoes to their destinations. He did not inquire about the morals or private life of the man he finally hired, the best man on the river at this or any other time: Mike Fink. He had to send to Natchez for Fink. As the story was told him, Mike Fink had just lost his own boat.

It seems that Mike had been doing very well with his own keelboat until about a month before, at which time he tied up at Natchez. Fink did not plan to stay there; he was anxious to get down to New Orleans where all his inherent meanness and mischievousness could find an outlet. He had been keeping out of the dives that lined the river banks, waiting to drink, gamble, and fight the town in New Orleans. Mike and his men tied up at Natchez about five o'clock in the afternoon. They lounged about on the dock, waiting for a cargo that Mike had arranged for. Mike, as usual, whiled away the dreary hours at target practice. By and by, he tired of sniping at floating driftwood and tin cups and looked about for some more inspiring mark.

There was a herd of pigs at the edge of the bluff several hundred feet away. Fink's eye lit on them, and he offered to bet one of his lieutenants that he could shoot the tails off every pig in the herd—and do it so gently that not one of them would know they had lost anything. The wager was made . . . and Mike, of course, won.

But every property has its owner, and on the following day a citizen of the town appeared with a court order summoning Mike Fink before the local bar of justice. Mike refused to answer the charge. The offended owner stamped off and came back with the police. Mike's men lined up behind him to a man. It looked as though the mayor would have to call out the local militia to back up his constabulary. One member of the force, however, an ex-riverman himself, had once poled under Mike. Presuming on his old friendship, he managed, after much persuasion and joshing, to get Mike to agree to appear.

Mike gave in, but on one condition. He claimed it gave him the dry heaves until he shook like a spavined horse if he had to walk for any distance on dry land. Therefore, he insisted that if justice was to be done, he would have to be transported to the courthouse on his boat. Then he sat back and waited for the authorities to get around that one.

They did. A few hours later a team of oxen, yoked to the longest, widest wagon that could be found, lumbered up to the wharf and prepared to take on Mike Fink, boat, crew, and all. Mike swallowed twice, but there was nothing he could do. He was cornered fair and square, and he knew it.

The historians of Natchez never did record exactly how the keelboat was lifted out of the water and deposited on the bed of the wagon, but when the feat was finally accomplished, Mike, proud even in defeat—or maybe actually tickled and willing to go along with the joke—took his place at the sweep oar, his crew assumed their regular poling positions, and the groaning oxen started off.

The road followed a steep hill that sloped up from the river to the main street where the courthouse was located. It was the busiest road in Natchez, and recent rains had beat the road-bed into a thick, slick paste. The oxen toiled on up, making slow, sliding headway. Occasionally, when it looked as though gravity and mud were going to have the best of the argument, the boatmen set their poles into the soft ground and heaving together got the animals onto firmer ground.

Halfway up the hill, Mike, having given the matter additional thought, decided to change his mind.

"Set poles!" he shouted.

In a flash every man jack had his pole braced and set. The oxen came to a sudden stop, unable to pull against the added opposition.

"Back her!" bawled Mike.

Back her they did and down the hill they went, wagon, barge, wild-eyed bellowing oxen, and all, for even a double yoke was no match for Mike's team of huskies. The police sent

159

the same ambassador, and the whole procedure of persuasion had to be repeated. Again Mike relented, and again the oxen set off.

This time Mike waited until the straining animals were about to breast the brim of the hill.

Then "Back her!" rang out again, and downhill went the wagon, clear to the wharf, with the police running alongside threatening and protesting. By this time, half the town was lined up along the hill, laughing and shouting encouragement, and Mike was enjoying every minute of it. The third time up, however, Mike stuck to the bargain and finally came into court. He had hardly finished reimbursing the pigs' owner, when a considerable body of leading citizens, hearing that Mike Fink had finally been hauled before a judge, burst into the court-room. They came prepared with a series of complaints ranging over a long period of time and covering a wide variety of sins. This was considerably more than Mike had bargained for. Facing the additional charges could mean life imprisonment or perhaps even hanging. Mike ordered his men back aboard the keelboat.

The swarm of indignant taxpayers surrounded the wagon and tried to board her, but the rivermen proved too much for them. Back down the hill went the wagon, this time at so fast a clip that the poor oxen arrived at the bottom dragging in the traces. Of all the assemblage at the dockside that day, they were probably the most relieved to see the keelboat refloated. That was the last time Mike answered for his pranks before the bar of human justice.

But this was not the end of the story. That night, while Mike and his men were at the local tavern, certain irate citizens came down to the river and sank the boat with all its cargo. When Mr. Montgomery's emissary arrived in Natchez five weeks later, he found Mike Fink still sitting in that tavern.

Fink came up the river to Cairo, and with him he brought ten of his original crew. He liked the look of the new boat, a beauty nine feet wide and sixty-five feet long. "She'll float on a heavy dew," Montgomery said, and Mike agreed with him.

This was the first time Montgomery had seen the much-fabled Fink. Montgomery, who was over six feet, had to look up into the face of this moccasined giant. The face he looked at was burned with sun and wind so that Mike seemed more Indian than white. He had on an Indian jacket, wore a long hunting knife in his belt, and carried a rifle. It didn't take more than a day to find out that his actions suited the stories about him, for he was as rough and salty as the frontier that made him, as crafty as the Indians he was forever fighting, as cruel and unpredictable as the wilderness in which he grew up and lived.

The boat was loaded with barrels of whiskey, cider, pork, and hogsheads of tobacco. The crew went aboard, and they floated out into the Mississippi. The three-month trip to New Orleans had started.

The men in his crew adored Mike Fink because he was unbeaten. The river never beat him, hunger never beat him, and drinking never beat him. He was successful. He talked big, fought big, ate and drank big, laughed and tore up the river dives and could play a practical joke better than anyone. Their Mike was never so happy as when he was engaged in a mad melee of flying fists and gouging thumbs—fighting just for the fun of it—or in battles with Indians or river pirates. When Mike was spoiling for a fight, it didn't matter much with whom he tangled, just so long as he tangled. But somehow he never tangled with his own men . . . or at least they did not stay with him if he did. When he played his practical jokes, it didn't much matter who got hurt or how badly, so long as he and his friends got their laughs.

Mike's crew was probably the best fed along the river, for he usually shot game as they went along the way. But on this trip game was scarce, and Mike found meat on the hoof in another form.

After they had passed Memphis, Mike noticed a flock of

sheep grazing in a pasture close to the river bank. As the keel-boat drew up alongside, one of the crew pointed out a quiet eddy well out of the main current close up under a low grassy bluff. Mike guided the boat in to shore and moored under the bluff. A farmer could be seen plowing off in the distance but close enough to hear any commotion from his bottom-land pasture. Mike and his men sat there looking at the sheep, their mouths watering, wondering how best to get some of that mutton aboard without paying.

Finally, an idea began to form in the crafty riverman's mind. There happened to be included in the cargo a consignment of Scotch snuff. Taking along a small bag of the pungent powder, Mike crept ashore and wriggling among the animals Indian fashion, rubbed it into the muzzles of as many ewes and fat lambs as he could catch. Then he crawled back to the boat and sent one of his men to summon the owner.

When the farmer got down to the river bank, he found seven or eight of his sheep acting in a strange way. The poor animals were dashing back and forth, bleating and shaking their heads, stopping now and then to rub their noses frantically into the ground, or to bat their heads against each other's flanks.

"What in the world's come over the critters?" cried the farmer.

Mike shifted his quid and spat into the Ohio. "Looks like the black murrain," he said.

The farmer's eyes popped. "Black murrain! What in the Sam Hill's that?"

Mike screwed up his eyes, and pointed off upstream.

"Mighty lot of that stuff hittin' sheep and cows up near Louisville. Heered tell just last night 'bout one party had fifty head caught it and skin me fer a wild b'ar effen every last one of them critters warn't dead by mornin'!"

While the boatmen looked on sympathetically, the distraught farmer swore and chewed his nails, wondering how in the world he was to save the flock. Someone came up with the bright suggestion of shooting the sick sheep before they could

spread the disease to the healthy ones. The farmer thought it
was a fine idea, but he couldn't see how anybody could possibly
shoot a lamb wildly running about in a large flock without hit-
ting one of the healthy sheep by mistake.

At that point the farmer found out that the man at the sweep
oar was none other than Mike Fink, the crack shot. He begged
him to shoot the sick sheep at once. Mike pretended to be reluctant. He opined he didn't like the idea of killing so many
fine-looking animals. But the farmer begged and pleaded, and
finally offered him twelve gallons of brandy as payment. It was
then that Mike agreed to perform the act of mercy.

He primed his gun, selected a fresh flint, and went to work.
As fast as one of the suffering animals was put out of its misery,
its carcass was flung over the bluff and into the placid water
of the eddy. When the last case of "murrain" had been disposed of, the brandy was handed over and the farmer went
home, thanking his lucky stars that Mike Fink had been on
hand to save the day. No sooner was he out of sight than the
dead sheep were hauled on board, the boat pushed off, and,
with wild whoops of triumph and joy, Mike and his men set off
down the Mississippi with a fresh supply of meat and plenty
of "aqua fortis" to wash it down.

They stopped at Nashville for a few days of relaxation in the
water-front dives. Here Mike indulged in his favorite sport. As
they waited for the river to be cleared of logs from a lumber
raft which had broken apart, Mike got up a contest to "shoot
for the beef." This, like other impromptu affairs, consisted of
gathering together all the good shots of the area and getting
someone to put up a young bull or a hogshead of whiskey as a
prize. A judge would be appointed, whose duty it was to decide
not only whose shot came closest to a given mark but which
marksman showed the most imagination and daring in planning his shot. Mike would usually shoot a small tin cup from
the head of a friend. This time, since he was up against a particularly strong opponent, he varied his routine by shooting the
cup from between his comrade's thighs, at a distance of over

one hundred yards. Mike's men took their hogshead of whiskey back to the boat for consumption.

And so it went with Mike Fink. These exploits were told and retold on the water front and from town to town. So gargantuan were Mike's actions, so almost unbelievable, that they were thought legendary even when they were not. And legendary exploits were attributed to him, which he was willing enough to take the credit for. They said that he rode a moose instead of a horse through the Nashville Trace. They said that going down the Mississippi on one trip he dove overboard for a swim and a she-wolf swam out from the shore to attack him. He grabbed her and held her under water until she drowned. They said that once when he was hungry, he had eaten a buffalo robe, but that it was New England rum and not the robe that had ruined his stomach. And so it went with Mike Fink during his lifetime.

And yet there was another Mike Fink, a man left out of the legends and wild yarns. A man who was a lover of nature, a half-savage dreamer who loved the river not only for its free and easy ways, but for the beauty of its waters, its bottom lands and forest highlands, and the glory of its sky.

When the boat was well out in the current and the spell at the sweep oar was over, this other man sat in the prow alone, ignoring the card games and wrestling matches and yarn spinning of his mates. There he sat, by day watching the wooded, rolling hills and rich pastures slip by, watching the life of the river's banks—the lumbering bear fishing the shallows, the watchful wildcat lapping at the water's edge, the quail and grouse and turkey, the soft-eyed does and many-antlered bucks dipping soft muzzles into the cool currents under the sheltering willows. There he sat at night and watched the fairy islands under the moon looming through the mists with their moss-draped trees gilded silver like the festooned masts of magic sailing ships.

And always there was the broad current, green-blue and rippling, and above the sweep of sky pillowed with cumulus or bristling with thunderheads. And the river soaked into his heart and mind, and the land grew into his soul. Out in the middle of the river, out of touch with the land that stretched on either side, this man was a man at peace—the ribald jester, the irrepressible upsetter of apple carts, was at peace with his world. His life stretched into his past and ahead of him, like the banks of the river, and in his terms it was an idyll.

The crew moved about quietly when this mood was on their chief, doing their best to keep out of his way. The keelboatmen made up the aristocracy of the river and Mike was supreme among this aristocracy. Besides being the best shot, he was the strongest, the roughest, and the cruelest. No doubt his men feared him, but they also respected him, and he had staunch friends among his followers, for he spoke their talk and fought their battles, sticking by them as loyally as they stuck by him.

Mike and his crew went past Natchez without fear and were not disturbed by the river pirates. The crew said this was because the pirate Murrel and his gang knew that Mike was in charge of the boat. When they arrived in New Orleans, Mike delivered his cargo, had his fill of the town, and then rounded up another cargo of sugar, salt, fabrics, and cooking utensils to go up the river. Then he went from saloon to saloon, bodily picking up his men and depositing them on the keelboat. With his crew divided evenly on either side of the boat, they shoved upstream from New Orleans by setting their poles in the bed of the river and walking slowly toward the stern. As each man reached the limit of his push, he disengaged his pole, lifted it, and ran forward to take his place at the bow. Mike stood governing the rudder and directing the crew. After three hours of this they were able to put up their sail and could sit back and take a drink from the whiskey kegs aboard. Mike was a hard taskmaster but his decisions were respected.

Up and down the Ohio and Mississippi rivers went Mike Fink, and somewhere along the line he picked up and befriended a homeless boy named Carpenter. Carpenter lived under Mike's protection for many years, going with him from one keelboat to another, becoming with every day that passed more like the son Mike had never had. Mike taught Carpenter everything he knew about the rivers and keelboating, about Indian fighting and hunting and shooting. When the boy grew into full manhood, he became Mike's trusted lieutenant and had Mike's affection and confidence. As the fullest expression of this, Carpenter was the only person Mike allowed to shoot the tin cup from his head. It was a breathtaking display of trust and confidence in each other's skill and good faith, and the two became famous for their trick along the entire length of the rivers.

The day finally came, however, when the paddle wheelers caught up with Mike Fink and the keelboats gradually went out of business. Mike blew his last pay as a keelboatman at Cave in Rock and Shawneetown, Illinois. When he sobered up, he took his aching head down to the riverside and stared at his world that had fallen down about him. The beautiful Ohio, the exciting Mississippi, his rivers, that had nourished and borne him through most of the years of his life, that had fed him and endured his wildest, most outlandish pranks, had suddenly turned fickle and heartless and had pushed him out of their lives forever.

These were the years when a good shot was always in demand and Mike soon signed up with a company trapping and trading for fur out of a fort near the mouth of the Yellowstone River. Young Carpenter went along with him and between the two of them they managed to raise as much havoc in the West as they ever had in the East. By this time Mike was well along in years though there wasn't a gray hair in his head to indicate that he was in his fifties. On the Yellowstone he probably found little to his liking. It was a different kind of river, this rapid, rushing, brawling, rock-filled Western river, and the country was unfriendly even in appearance. He longed for the feel of a keelboat under his feet and the sight of morning mist rising over the banks of the Muskingum. But those days were dead and gone, and their memory lay at the bottom of a bottle. More and more, Mike turned to those memories with the aid of plenty of whiskey, trying to change the unhappy present into the idyllic past. In his growing demand for this escape from the Yellowstone back to the Ohio and the Mississippi, he became something of a nuisance at the fort; he had an unpleasant habit of always carrying his rifle with him when he came to trade for whiskey.

There was a prohibition against drinking on government posts, and Mike finally had a falling out with the commandant who ordered him off the premises. Mike and Carpenter retired to a cave where the old man drank himself from one stupor into another, brooding and sulking and sighing for the good old days when he was chief cock of the walk along the Ohio and Mississippi.

Perhaps it was the incessant drinking bouts and the filthy conditions of the cave, but whatever happened, there was a violent quarrel and the two men split up. Carpenter moved out of the cave and into his own hut; Mike rolled a stone over the entrance to his burrow and disappeared from the sight of man like a hibernating bear.

With the spring thaw, Mike emerged from his hide-out. He was lonely and remorseful and longed for a reconciliation. After a good deal of hemming and hawing, Mike offered to meet Carpenter halfway and let bygones be bygones. A group of friends gathered about the mouth of Mike's cave to celebrate the reunion. Jugs and cans were passed from hand to hand. Talk and boasting went on and on. There were songs and yarns and wrestling matches, shouted brags, and boasts. Finally, as a climax to the shindig, Mike suggested that he and Carpenter perform their famous shooting stunt.

By this time both men were considerably foggy. But a little hard liquor had never kept a "half hoss, half alligator" down, so the guns were loaded and the two took up positions facing each other about fifty yards apart. In a generous mood, Mike granted Carpenter the first shot. He placed the cup on his head and stood there grinning from ear to ear. Carpenter raised his rifle unsteadily, trying to take aim through the whiskey fumes. The onlookers laughed and joked, speculating about how much Mike's hide would bring on the market in St. Louis. After a long spell of weaving and sighting, Carpenter fired.

The cup flew into the air, but the grin faded from Mike's face. He stood stock still, staring at Carpenter, with a thin line of blood trickling down the side of his face. Too tight to notice that he had grazed Mike's scalp, Carpenter took his place as the target and waited for Mike's shot.

Mike picked up his gun and took careful aim. The piece was held to his shoulder as though it were in a vise. To the onlookers it seemed not to waver even the fraction of an inch.

Mike fired. A second later Carpenter fell dead, Mike's bullet in his brain. The men went off in suddenly sober groups. Mike retired to his cave.

At the fort, the talk was all for bringing Mike to trial. Some of the trappers were willing to give him the benefit of the doubt, claiming bad aim due to the influence of alcohol. There were others, however, who insisted that Mike Fink had never missed a shot in his life, drunk or sober—unless he meant to!

The loudest of these others was a gunsmith named Talbot who was particularly strong in his denunciations of Fink as a murderer. Eventually Talbot's remarks got to the cave and roused Mike to action.

One morning Talbot looked out through the door of his shop to see Mike approaching. He was thin and run down, for he had been living on whiskey ever since the tragic shooting. He was unsteady on his feet, and he had with him his constant companion, his rifle.

Talbot snatched up a brace of pistols and warned Mike to stay away. Mike advanced slowly, pleading his innocence, swearing that he loved Carpenter like a son, that the shooting was accidental. Talbot, gibbering with fear, kept warning Mike off, and Mike kept stumbling forward, begging Talbot to believe him.

When Mike was just outside the shop, Talbot threatened to fire if he passed over the threshold. Unheeding, Mike moved forward. All this time his gun had not been raised, not once lifted in any way. Talbot fired. Mike fell forward. He died a few minutes later, still protesting his innocence.

So ended Mike Fink, far from his beloved river, broken and tragic, his grave unmarked and since forgotten. Behind the legend and the myth is the man, brutal and violent as the frontier that made him, in his final scenes lost and pathetic, like the driftwood of a passing flood left to rot on the mud flats.

A Red Berry and Two Hills of Snow

You've heard people remark on seeing a lovely child: "How I'd like to take you home with me!" You've probably said it yourself, and more than once. And you've probably meant it too. This feeling comes from down deep inside us, from the need to cradle and adore a child, even the offspring of an enemy. There are countless stories about gypsies and how they carried some child away. The Wee Folk are constantly accused of luring children to their enchanted abode. In fable and song and fairy tale we see this story repeated over and over again. But this legend is, I think, different from the others.

JOHN AND Alice Summers had a little girl named Mary. By the time this little girl was four years old, everyone was calling her "Star" because of her bright, shining eyes. Her hair was black as darkest night, her skin snow-white, and her eyes a bright shining blue. So she became Star to everyone.

John and Alice Summers had lived on the River Genesee for five years. Soon after their wedding, before Star was born, they went west and settled in what was then dangerous Indian country. However, the Indians were moving farther and farther west and by the time Star was four years old, they seldom saw any redskins except for those who had taken on the white ways.

Star was very lonesome until a young boy of six years came to live nearby. His parents were pioneers too. The families were friendly and the children spent many happy hours playing in the clearing or running about along the banks of the nearby river. Star's playmate was named James Ganes. Their favorite game was one of hide-and-seek. Star would hide while

James closed his eyes, for as long as it took him to call out a rhyme his father had taught him. This rhyme fitted their game particularly well:

"Twinkle, twinkle, little star,
How I wonder where you are!"

He would shout the last few words, then open his eyes and search. Both children could be heard screaming with delight when he found her.

One afternoon the children were playing this game and strayed some distance from the clearing to a small creek which flowed into the river. Star hid and before James could finish his poem, a heavy downpour and darkness fell unexpectedly. James called aloud for Star, but she did not answer him. The cloudburst had caused the creek to become full of rushing water and the little boy thought that she had fallen in. He ran, screaming for help.

After searching long on this and many other days, the parents gave up hope of finding little Star again. John and Alice Summers were almost crazed with grief. For a time, the neighbors took care of them, and then allowing that hope was gone, the Summers went about their work with heavy hearts. The years passed, but they did not forget, nor were they blessed with another child.

John Summers had one added burden to bear, for his wife Alice never did accept the death of little Star as a fact. She would talk about the possibilities of the child living. John would answer her patiently, "Turn it from your mind, Alice. There is no good in thinking this way." Her health had never been good since that black day of many years ago.

One of the few joys of Alice's life were the visits of a fur trader, Alistair McGreggar, a man much loved by all the pioneers. Of all the hunters, soldiers of fortune, and emigrants that passed through this pioneer settlement, only McGreggar won everyone's heart. He had a burr to his speech that matched his name, and he was a sensitive man and an honest one. He moved freely among the Indians and lived among them with honor. Always he carried his bagpipes. These had proved a passport to the Indian tribes, for the wild, leaping melodies of the chanter and the stirring monotone of his drones moved the Indians to feelings of peace and reverence, and made them more religious, they had told him, than any preaching. It need not be stated that McGreggar always left the tribe he was visiting with their finest furs.

He came to the Summers home twice yearly, stopping a few days each time. His stories and his music moved Alice from the lethargy in which she existed; they amused her and took her mind from the tragedy of Star. McGreggar, of course, knew the story of the little girl who had disappeared. He had often talked to John Summers about it. As a matter of fact, he was the only one who had ever said to John Summers, "I know Alice thinks she lives. If she were alive, I would have come across her. If she did not drown that day and the wild beasts did not eat her, if she did not die from exposure, then she would have been found by some Indian tribe. I never heard of a little white girl being among any in this area."

One year, Alistair McGreggar did not come to pay his annual visit. Spring came, and again fall, but no Alistair. James Ganes, now a lad of sixteen years, was the only person to whom Alice now responded. The boy had never ceased to feel guilty about the disappearance of his little friend Star. He spent much time at the Summers's house and helped the aging John with many duties that ordinarily would have been his wife's.

It was the following spring when James Ganes was hailed from the forest and Alistair McGreggar came forth. The two men, the old trader and the young lad, went together to the Summers's. It was a night for talking and music. Alistair said he had a message for some family along the Genesee River, and he offered to tell them what it was. His eye on Alice, he began: "In my travels I have often by-passed the hut of old Chief Skenondah. He would not trade with me and was once a chief warmaker on all white men. This year he sought me out to give this message to some family. I am to tell this family of two hills of snow between which grows a berry, red as the setting sun. The family who comes to claim it shall have it."

Alice Summers rose from her chair, dropped her knitting needles to clasp her hands to her bosom. Her eyes stared wildly at McGreggar before she fell to the floor in a faint.

After the excitement of reviving her and making her comfortable was over, they sat once again before the fire. "It's Star, my Star," she whispered. How can you be sure? her husband and the others wanted to know. She was sure and would have gone out into the night immediately, had they not restrained her.

"I will go for her," said James Ganes. "It is only right that I find her. How can I go?"

"I will go and get her immediately. Tell me where," shouted John Summers.

"No," said Alistair, "I think the young lad should go. Old Skenondah is a romantic. If the young lad goes, he is less likely to change his mind. Take my advice, John, let the young lad go. I am wise in the thinking of the red man."

And so it was decided. Young Ganes, outfitted by McGreggar for his ordeal, with explicit instructions as to trails and stopping points, started into the wilderness next day. His way grew more and more difficult, for the Indians had moved into ever wilder country to escape the encroaching white habitations.

The young man was romantic and no knight ever went on a quest with a stronger image of beauty or burden of guilt than this young hunter. Many a quiet night would find him looking up at the stars and whispering that little poem of his childhood, "Twinkle, twinkle, little star, how I wonder where you are." He did not add although his heart was hopeful, "If you are." Loneliness lay heavily on his heart.

It was on the afternoon of the third day that he came to the landmark McGreggar had directed him to, the mark that told him that he was in the land of the old Indian chief. It was a great oak tree, from which hung hundreds of scalps, trophies of the old chief and his tribe. From here, he had to proceed on foot to a thick forest, cutting his own trail. He made a wide tether for his horse and plunged into the underbrush.

At night he could hear the wildcats weeping, like grief-stricken women; the owls and night birds called to each other with news of the intruder. Fearful as he was, he continued to go forward. At dawn, he came to a clearing beside a lovely lake. Stumbling, he ascended a small hill, at the summit of which sat a lonely wigwam.

There by the side of the tent, he saw a newly dug grave. He staggered to the mound of fresh earth, and the awareness that this grave was his journey's fulfillment filled him with bitter grief. Exhausted, disappointed, and despairing, he fell across the grave and wept. Sleep finally overcame him.

When he woke up, he looked around and saw a very old Indian, his leather face creased with hundreds of wrinkles, stonily gazing at him. He rose to his feet and would have spoken, but the old Indian said in good English, "You weep as a woman."

The young man could only answer brokenly, "I had come to claim the red berry that grows between two hills of snow." And he turned to gaze once more at the newly dug grave.

The old chief spoke again. "It is Half Moon, my own daughter, who lies there. Shooting Star was as a sister to her. Do you claim this maiden for your own?"

James had been well instructed by McGreggar and he said in formal speech, "I have come to claim two hills of snow between which grows a berry, red as the setting sun."

The old chief rose and went inside the teepee. He emerged, followed by a fair-complexioned girl. Her black hair was combed back tightly, as was the Indian fashion, and fell in two long braids over each shoulder. Her eyes were as bright as the stars. James's heart leaped at her beauty and if before he had loved an idea, he now loved a reality. But this was not enough for Old Skenondah.

James did not doubt for a minute that she was his old play-

177

mate, but Skenondah gave him proof. He ripped the blouse front of the maiden, showing her white breasts, between which a small round birthmark, as red and as beautiful as any ruby, stood out. Then the chief led her by the hand to the young man.

The old chief stepped back and gazed upon the two young people. "I promised my daughter she should go to her own people. Take her. I go to the setting sun."

The young girl began to weep, for she knew what he meant to do, and he had been good to her. Yet she stood unmoving by the side of young James Ganes as the old chief went about his preparations. First, the old man picked up two nearby bags that were filled with stones. He carried these slowly, for they were heavy, to a canoe that was half out of the water on the shore. He put several large stones in the canoe, tied the two bags on either side of his heavy, old body, entered the canoe and pushed it out into the lake. As they watched, he slowly paddled toward the lake center. The canoe turned broadside to the young people. They saw him swing his tomahawk and splinter the frail birch bottom of the canoe. Once again he paddled forward, singing his death song. The boat slowly sank, deeper and deeper, until finally only two white paddles floated on the calm, blue water.

John Tabor, Whaler

I don't know why this should be so, but fishing seems to bring out the liar in man. I have seen people stretch the size of a fish they have caught—or almost caught—from six inches to a foot and a half or more. And when the talk is of whales . . . well, maybe the larger the quarry the more fantastic the tale. After all, the whale is a pretty fantastic creature to begin with.

FOLLOWING the American Revolution, American whaling ships voyaged from Greenland to the South Pacific. The trips were so uncomfortable and arduous, the work so hard and dangerous that, as in present-day combat fighting, youth was essential to those who went out on the long voyages.

New England whaling ships dropped anchor all over the world: New Guinea, the Solomons, the Admiralties and even the Sandwich Islands (which we now call Hawaii). Sealskins, *bêche-de-mer*, edible birds' nests, turtle shells, sandalwood, and sea bird guano made up a part of the cargoes that they brought back, but it was the whale oil, whale bone, whalemeat and ambergris which brought in enormous revenues.

To many young men of New Bedford the thought of adventure on a whaling ship proved irresistible. Among them was young John Tabor. He would not be dissuaded by the warnings of family or friends, and the stories of ill treatment aboard the vessels or the general difficulties facing a young novice seemed nothing to him. Tabor was accustomed to fending for himself; his father had died when he was eight years old and his mother, unable to support her large family, had hired the boy out to a farmer near Boston. Here we find John Tabor doing a man's work by the time he was nine. Even his play was practical. When he went swimming, he clammed for extra money; if he went on a picnic, he also picked cranberries or blackberries to sell. This money he always sent back to his mother. Perhaps he would have remained a farmer and eventually owned his own farm, but, one day when he was working in the field, his employer struck him in the face for an impertinence. Young Tabor threw down his hoe and immediately ran away. The tales he had heard as a child on the New Bedford wharves made him determined to ship on a whaler. Nothing his mother nor brothers said could change his mind.

Young John looked through the *New Bedford Times* and found this advertisement:

> WANTED, WHALERS: Fifty stout young men, Americans, wanted for whaling ship fitting out for South Pacific fisheries. Only industrious young men taken. Superior chances for advancement. Outfits to amount of $50.00 furnished each individual. Persons willing to avail themselves of opportunity to see world and participate in percentage business should make application to Ship CHARLES W. MORGAN.

Tabor found the ship at the New Bedford dock, ready for sea. He did not know that the crew was incomplete and that the captain was even then waiting for a press gang to bring in a full complement. The captain was quite willing to take on the fifteen-year-old Tabor but explained to him that there were no wages as whalers were expected to share in the profits. Tabor agreed with alacrity, thinking it fair to gamble for a good or poor voyage.

Once the ship was out to sea and he had survived his first seasickness, John found himself in a company of some thirty-five men. Some of these, like himself, thought to see the world and gain adventure, a few ambitious ones planned in time to own whaling ships of their own, about twenty-five were experienced whalers, although none of them were more than twenty-eight years old. Six were young farmer lads who had been pressed in one of the local taverns. All in all, it was a usual crew, including cook, carpenter, blacksmith, cooper, and boat steerer.

After leaving the harbor, the captain called the crew forward and laid down the rules of the voyage. He told them they had come to work hard, catch whales, and, he hoped, get back home in good time. Swearing lustily, the captain dismissed his men with the warning that under no circumstances would he tolerate profanity aboard his vessel.

Tabor, with the other greenhorns, had to learn how to row, handle the oars, trim the sails, and use paddles. Every day there was practice in lowering the boats. Tabor, who was a likeable young lad, ingratiated himself with the old-timers and received much valuable instruction from them.

The ship had been out a full month when one of the four lookouts called, "There she blows! Blo-o-o-ws! There she breaches!" Tabor, rushing to the rail, was in time to see the whale leap high and land on his back in the water with a slap that resounded for miles around. The boats were ready, and everything was prepared for the chase. Much as he would have liked to join the boat crew, Tabor was forced to stay aboard the vessel and watch. To his surprise, the boats were not immediately lowered but stayed on the *Morgan* and the whale disappeared. He was disappointed until one of the men explained that whales often submerge for as long as an hour once they discover they have been spotted.

Sure enough, the whale finally rose to the surface, spouting about once every minute. Two boats were lowered, the men immediately starting to pull on their oars. Tabor's informant exclaimed excitedly, "That's a big one! He'll be a hard customer to handle!"

The two boats raced to reach the whale, which was cruising at a speed of about three miles an hour. The backs of the rowers were to the whale and the men did not turn to look in the direction in which the boatheader, at the tiller, was directing them. It would have been bad whaling form to glance around and their first knowledge of nearness to their prey came when the harpooner received his command. Tabor heard the mate shouting to the harpooner, "Stand! Let him have it!"

On command, the harpooner shipped his oars, got to his feet and tossed his first iron. Tabor could see him throwing a second harpoon, after which he quickly started to run aft at the same time the boatheader dropped the tiller and ran forward. The harpooner took over the tiller and tended to the tow lines, which were about one hundred fathoms long. The boatheader took his proper place in the bow of the boat, readying himself to throw the killing lance. The two men exhibited superb balance as they passed each other on the run in the little boat.

The harpoon, as Tabor knew from having tried unsuccessfully to handle it, was a heavy, unwieldy instrument about eleven feet long and as thick as a man's wrist. From a distance the harpooner seemed to throw it with ease. As soon as the whale felt the painful shock of the harpoon's blow, he took a violent plunge in reaction, then another plunge from the second blow. The little whaleboat suddenly began to tear along the surface of the water in the "Nantucket sleigh ride." The boatmen had their oars peaked, ready for use, resting at an acute angle over the gunwales. They were holding on for all they were worth in order to stay in the boat as it went over the waves at a speed of fifteen knots an hour, throwing spray out on both sides.

Finally the whale tired, and the little boat moved in under its own power for the kill.

The linesman hurled his weapon and the whale began to bleed. As the sea grew red around the beast, Tabor knew the whale was done for. Due to the nonvalvular structure of a whale's blood vessels, his lifeblood drains swiftly away once bleeding starts. The sea for yards around the monster was crimson. Finally he was so tired that the boat was able to come in close. Once again the linesman struck, now behind the pectoral fins. The whale upended in the pond of his own red blood, creating a tremendous spray. Then swimming furiously in rapidly narrowing circles he came into view. He spouted only once and the spout was scarlet. His heart had burst.

The whaling boat stayed a little distance from the whale for about an hour longer. Then the ship itself came up and took the whale alongside. As the crew lashed the whale to the ship, it was pulled on its side by the animal's weight. The whale was about seventy-five feet long and reached from the vessel's fore chain to her mizzen.

Since this was a right whale, it floated by itself, and no air had to be pumped into it. On deck, preparations were immediately under way to cut the whale into blubber. It was the harpooner's job to stand on top of the slippery body and hook into the first piece. Tabor, watching anxiously, thought it was extremely lucky that the sea was not heavy; sharks, attracted by the whale's blood, were greedily swimming around the ship and would have made short work of the harpooner if he had slipped.

This part of whaling was an untidy business, full of hard and difficult work. Tabor worked on the blubber with the others. He became oil-soaked and blood-spattered. He waded in blood. The whole ship seemed bathed in oil and blood, the decks were slippery with it, the men were covered with it. The oil was in Tabor's hair, in his ears, under his fingernails, soaked into his shoes and clothing. The odor of boiling blubber grew so unbearable that Tabor felt very sick. He received little sympathy from the old-timers who had been on the chase and accepted the drudgery and oil and blood as part of their jobs.

During the next few weeks, several whales were sighted. One day they fastened to a whale but it came on to blow and she got loose. Once they fastened to a cow and calf. They killed the cow but lost her as she went off spouting blood. In the next two months, their average was four right whales lost, three saved. The men considered this a good betting average and spirits were high.

All of this took place in the South Atlantic. Finally, having tried out the whales that were caught, the *Charles W. Morgan* put into Rio de Janeiro and sold off eighty barrels of whale oil. Here the ship took on stores and headed for Cape Horn and the Pacific Ocean. The voyage to the Horn was a mild one with weather fair or calm. The men sat around talking, making spun yarn, and braiding rope yarn together. They polished their equipment and ground harpoons and lances until they were sharp enough to cut a hair. They made knickknacks out of shells and whales' teeth. One of the old-timers taught Tabor how to scrimshaw. He made beautiful designs on two whales' teeth. On one he carved and etched the picture of a beautiful girl dancing, putting in colors with red, blue, and green Indian ink. On the second tooth he etched a picture of their ship under full sail. He did his carving with a jackknife and etched in the design with a sail needle. He smoothed down the ivories with the ship's grindstone and when the design was finished gave his work a high polish by using wood ashes and the palm of his hand for many hours on end. Many of the men made corset stays for their girl friends at home, etching on them touching or suggestive designs.

The ship had not seen a whale for three months when one day a sperm bull was sighted. Tabor was amazed at its size. They immediately lowered four boats. The whale proved to be a fighter, like most sperm whales. Tabor, who had now advanced to the position of rower, knew black fear as the harpooned animal rushed the boat. However, the boatheader and the men pulled away on their oars with a will, and they were lucky to escape the mad rush.

What a ride this whale gave them! Finally, he was lashed to the ship. So great was his size that cutting into him took several days. He provided a nice haul in sperm oil and whalebone. Since sperm oil and bone commanded a good high price, the men worked willingly enough to try him out.

This was the only excitement before the ship rounded the Horn. The trip around the Horn was uneventful. Tempers were short and there were several incidents aboard. After three months of solitude, the men grew bored with each other and with each other's stories. Two of the men grew rebellious to the point where they had to be put in irons. The weather alternated between days of severe gale and complete calm. Fresh food had almost given out; fish and dried beef began to grow monotonous.

Two weeks after rounding the Horn, the larder of the *Morgan* received an unexpected lift. The men were delighted to sight another ship on the horizon. She was the whaler *Emerald*, out of Salem, bound for home. The two ships hailed each other and made ready to gam. It was necessary for a complete boat crew to leave the ship together in order to be prepared to take a whale if one appeared. Thus, two complete crews, including the boat steerers, prepared to go to the *Emerald*. The skipper stood in one of them; it would have been beneath the dignity of his position as captain to sit, so he attempted a casual air by keeping both hands in his trouser pockets. His position was made even more precarious when the boat steerer's twenty-eight-foot oar hit him now and then in the small of his back. In front, his knees were tapped at regular intervals by the after oar. Finally the boat was brought safely alongside the *Emerald*.

On board the *Emerald* they were treated to foods of which Tabor had heard but never before tasted or seen: poi, breadfruit, and other exotic foods from Pacific islands. The *Morgan's* crew returned to their ship with a welcome variety of fresh provisions.

As the voyage continued, six sperm whales were brought in. In the sixth whale, they found 180 pounds of ambergris. Since this was sold for approximately two hundred dollars a pound, it was worth as much as their entire haul to date.

At last they put into port, for the first time in seven months, at the Hawaiian Islands. Because of the lack of wind, the ship stayed in port nine days, and the men were able to go ashore. On the ninth day, the *Morgan* left, completely stored with food, but . . . she did not leave with John Tabor aboard.

187

What happened to John Tabor was a mystery; he had been drinking with the men ashore one night when he suddenly disappeared. A search was made for him but he was nowhere to be found, and the ship finally left without him. Among themselves, the men decided that like many another whaler he had probably found a native princess and would never return to New England.

Now, it is a strange but true fact that when the *Charles W. Morgan* returned to New Bedford, John Tabor was at the dock waiting for her. This is the story he told, and a strange, miraculous one it was:

Tabor swore that he was standing on the beach at Hawaii that last night when he heard a whale breach not far offshore. Suddenly a little native man, whose hair was white and long, appeared beside Tabor. He commanded him to get into his boat and go with him after the whale. Thinking this was a chance to make a great personal killing, Tabor did as the old man asked.

They jumped into a small Hawaiian surfboat and the old man took up the oars. The boat raced over the water at an amazing speed, approaching a sperm whale that could be seen by moonlight lying quietly in the sea. There was a harpoon in the bottom of the boat. Tabor picked it up and would have thrown it, but the little old man seized the harpoon and threw it into the back of the whale. Then seizing Tabor with amazing strength, he lifted him high above his head, hoisted him out of the boat onto the whale's back, crying, "Hold fast, Tabor! Stick on like death, Tabor!" The harpoon was in front of Tabor, whose instinct was to grab it, but before he could do so, the little old man jumped onto the whale in front of him and seized the harpoon himself. The whale started off with the speed of lightning. All Tabor could do was hold onto the pants of the little old man, who, believe it or not, was standing on the whale's back, balancing himself with his knees. Tabor clung desperately to the seat of the old man's pants.

All night long they went over the waves and the next day

and the next, until Tabor was dizzy from lack of food. At sunrise the third morning the little old man shouted, "Land ho!" Tabor raised his tired head and was startled into wakefulness when he realized they were whizzing by Nantucket. The whale turned north and entered Buzzards Bay. At New Bedford, it hit the beach so fast that it smashed into the rotting hulk of a ship which had gone aground many years before. So great was the impact that the old man flew head foremost over the wrecked ship, leaving the entire seat of his pants in Tabor's hands. Tabor lost consciousness. When he came to, he was alone on the beach, and both the whale and the little old man had disappeared.

Tabor swore to the truth of this tale and it is a fact that he did suddenly appear in the town from the beach one day. It is also a fact that it would have been extremely difficult for him to have got back to New Bedford first on another ship, since the *Charles W. Morgan* had come directly home from Hawaii, without stopping enroute for further whaling.

Tabor himself swore the tale was true. Yet in later years he complained bitterly, not that people doubted his story, but that they believed it so completely he never again got a berth on a whaling ship.

American Family Westward

*I have traveled this country by plane, by train, by car—
and in my younger days on foot with my guitar slung
over my shoulder. I know its vastness well and I
realize what it must have been like to cross it a
hundred years or so ago. Understanding the dangers
and discomforts of that time, I think of the old-timers
I have met who could still remember those days. I
recall their wrinkled faces, their trembling hands,
and I think of them as they were in their youth, full
of vitality and bravery, the elements that made our
country.*

I N THE East, politicians vacillated. Peter Hardeman Burnett, the struggling young lawyer, hated politicians and
wished to become one. He even made up this little verse,
about a typical politician, that got into the *Nashville Press*:

> *He wobbled in, he wobbled out,*
> *Until he left the mind in doubt*
> *Whether the snake that made the track*
> *Was going south or coming back.*

Although educational opportunities were scant in Nashville,
Tennessee, where he had been born in 1807, Peter made the
most of those that came his way. However, the rules he lived
by came, not from books but from the laws laid down by his
maternal grandfather, Thomas Hardeman. Old Hardeman had
told his grandson that only three precepts were necessary to
make a man successful: "First, pay your honest debts. Second,
never disgrace your family. Third, help your honest and industrious kin." The memory of his grandfather stood Peter Burnett
in good stead many times. The memories of the hardness of his
early days when clothing was homespun, tea nonexistent except

193

for the root of the sassafras, and parched corn meal the sole food for weeks on end, kept him seeking for wealth when otherwise he might have given up.

He was not only a hard-working man but a lucky one, for in 1828 he married Harriet W. Rogers, with whom he was passionately in love. They were married in August of that year and devoted the next twelve years to each other and to raising their six children.

Perhaps Peter Burnett would have continued as a hard-working, successful young lawyer in western Missouri, where they had settled, had not Harriet become ill. The doctor became a daily caller at the Burnett house, but he could not make a diagnosis. Harriet had "the miseries." Peter brooded about her condition.

One day he waylaid the doctor with an idea. "Doctor," he said, "before Harriet took to bed I was thinking of moving west. Harriet and I talked about it and we thought maybe California, maybe farther north. We figured that now the Oregon Territory is opening up to settlers, there would be plenty of opportunity for a lawyer. What do you think a change of scenery would do to my wife, doctor?"

The doctor pondered a moment and gave a good professional answer, "Now, Mr. Burnett, your wife's condition can't improve overnight. You must be patient. It certainly doesn't call for such a drastic move as going to the Oregon Territory."

"Now what I'm asking you is would a trip perk her up, maybe? You say there's nothing organically wrong with her. You don't know what's wrong with her, and you can't help her. Maybe a change of scenery would do it."

The doctor was a philosopher, "Maybe a trip will do it. It may kill her, it may cure her. If you're bent on moving on and she wants to go, take a chance, by all means take a chance."

Burnett, a man of immediate action and great enthusiasms, crashed into the house shouting, "Harriet! Get up! You have to hurry—we're going to Oregon! You're going to get well!"

Harriet did get up, and on May 8, 1843, she helped Peter

194

and the children hitch up two ox wagons with four yoke of oxen, the small horse wagon with two mares. She checked the provisions, tied two mules onto the rear of the procession, counted the children to be sure they were all present, tucked her arm in Peter Burnett's, and set out from western Missouri for the wagon train rendezvous, which was set up twelve miles west of Independence. On the seat beside her she had *Conant's Guide to the West.*

No guide ever prepared the pioneers for their first view of a wagon rendezvous. Campfires lighted the prairies for miles, and beside each campfire were wagons and all the earthly possessions of their owners. In the flickering glow, if you walked from group to group, you could make out the words "For Oregon" and "Over the Rockies" painted haphazardly on this wagon and that. This was the first Oregon migration on a big co-operative scale.

Independence was used to wagon trains and expeditions going west (the Santa Fe Trail began at Independence) and to Frémont's military parties provisioning there, but there was nothing like the whooping and bragging and praying of these travelers. The storekeepers were the happiest members of the community—selling provisions and giving free advice to open-mouthed customers. Quite incidentally, they made more profit in this month of May, 1843, than in the rest of the entire year before or after. "You would think they was going to the Promised Land," one cynical storekeeper said.

When Harriet and Peter and their children arrived, there were already 875 people gathered in over two hundred wagons. They waited and waited—and waiting, they visited each other and became acquainted. There was little talk of organization, for they had a lot to learn about traveling in wagon trains. And there were fears: about the Indians, about wild beasts, about starvation. Stories were rife. Everybody had heard something of a fearful nature, but everybody had hope.

At dawn of the starting day, Harriet and Peter carefully checked their wagons and livestock, settled the children in their respective places, and joined the procession slowly moving out onto the prairie. Peter stood up in their lead wagon to look back. For miles, as far as he could see, there was a line of wagons with white covers, with horsemen dashing here and there, men traveling on foot beside their wagons, and small groups of cattle.

Neither the men nor the cattle were trail broken—but it was the cattle that gave immediate trouble. After a few hours of slow progress along the dusty trail, the cows wanted to go home. So did lots of their owners though they didn't admit it. The poor cattle; all up and down the caravan of cumbersome wagons frantic men galloped back and forth, nudging straying beasts back into line, urging them forward with prods and curses. Some of the more domesticated cows just lay down in the middle of the trail as they would have done in their own pastures. The oncoming wagons went around them, and owners stopped beside them and attempted to move them.

The families had a difficult time of it. The first few hours on the road felt like days and weeks to many of the wives and children who sat swaying and bumping on the high wagons. Unused to traveling, Harriet gritted her teeth and did not complain. Like many of the other women she was already homesick for friends and familiar places left behind. Yet whatever portion of the wagon train would have turned back from the glories of the Golden West if a vote had been taken at that moment, Harriet would not have been one of them.

There was constant argument over guard duty, over grazing places for the stock, over mistakes in judgment. Peter Burnett's precise legal mind rebelled against the quibbling and quarreling. He stood quiet and apart. Each man should have met the daily challenge of pioneer life not as an individual but as part of a large group. Peter would have liked to organize, but tempers were too quick and he did not interfere.

Tempers were particularly frayed because, in spite of the many talents of this worthy aggregation, there was no one trained in the art of reconnoitering. On May 24, for instance, the entire group spent all the hours of the day till long after dusk letting the wagons down a difficult creek bank one by one. Burnett was at the end of the wagon train. He came up at dusk and waited his turn. Restless, he walked a few hundred yards farther and found there an excellent ford. If someone had ridden ahead to look at the trail, the wagon train might have gotten across in much less time. Burnett took the ford and, being a man used to holding his peace, said nothing to the others.

One evening, Harriet Burnett was fixing a dinner of biscuits, potatoes, and a thick aromatic meat stew. Just as she was ladling out great portions for her lively brood, she noticed some men standing in the shadows of her big wagon. Flushed with the exertion of cooking and pleased with the result, she called out, "If you haven't et, come on up to the fire and help yourselves. We've aplenty."

Eight hungry men lurched forward and gorged themselves.

The next night they appeared as the cover came off the pot. This time they brought friends and so Harriet and Peter found themselves running a free eats establishment. Always the hospitable soul, Harriet was embarrassed about turning these dinner guests away, but it was obvious that if she continued to play hostess to a great party that increased nightly, she would soon be left without provisions.

Peter watched for some four nights. On the fifth night he made Harriet stay in the wagon and cooked the dinner himself. He cooked only enough for his family, served them, and sat down to eat with nary a look to right or left at his audience. Five minutes of silent munching was all that the assembly needed to take the hint that the party was over and that they had better look elsewhere for a handout . . . or as a desperate measure resort to cooking their own dinners.

Burnett and others in the caravan were very relieved when their guide, Captain Gant, joined them at the Kansas River. Captain Gant proved to have a contagious sense of humor, a commodity sorely needed by the travelers. Rumor had it that before he joined them, the captain had been cashiered out of the United States Army for padding payrolls. To many, his high spirits compensated for his reputed lack of character. It was certainly true that he was a seasoned veteran of several journeys overland to the Pacific by way of the Oregon Trail. With his arrival, a sense of well-being pervaded the wagon train.

The caravan proceeded under Captain Gant's direction to the ferry crossing on the banks of the Kansas. Here a Frenchman called "Papa" greeted them.

"How many wagons are there?" Papa asked in a thick French accent.

Captain Gant and Peter Burnett, who had become good friends, rode up to him. "Two hundred and three wagons," said the captain.

"Cost you four hundred six dollars to ferry you across. Two dollars a wagon, money in advance, m'sieu, *s'il vous plaît*."

"You're supposed to be a ferryman, not a highway robber," Burnett said sarcastically.

Gant used methods of diplomacy obviously learned in the army. He shouted, "Listen to me, you crazy Frenchman. We're United States citizens, and you have to ferry us across at a reasonable price. Your price insults us."

"My ferry will not be insulted by four hundred six dollars. I do not equivocate, *mon capitaine*. I do not argue. My price, it is set. If you do not like it, you turn around and return to your homes, or you swim across the river. As for me, I would better sit and drink *vin ordinaire* and think about life than work myself with two hundred three wagons. This is a lot of wagons, m'sieu. Indeed, as I think, four hundred six dollars is not enough for such effort. . . ."

As the Frenchman waved his arms in true Gallic fashion, the

two horsemen turned from him and galloped back to the wagons, Gant deliberately kicking dirt in the ferryman's face as he spun around.

"Why don't we see how deep the river is?" Burnett suggested. "Maybe we can ford it."

"Don't be a fool," Gant replied. "We're not Israelites and this isn't the Red Sea. I know this river; it's impossible to ford for over two hundred miles upstream."

"Well, what do we do?" Burnett rejoined testily. "Do we give the Frenchman what he asks? Do we do what he tells us and go back to Missouri?"

Gant pondered for a moment. "Well, we'll have to build ourselves a couple of rafts. It's the only way to get across."

By this time, a number of men had ridden up to see what the delay meant and to inquire how the wagons were to cross the river. Standing up in his stirrups, Gant cupped his hands around his mouth and called out the situation to them. "That no-good Frenchman wants four hundred and six dollars to take us across the river. That's too much money. I say we don't give it to him. We can build our own rafts and ferry ourselves across the river. What do you say?"

Astounded murmuring at the Frenchman's price turned into a rousing "Yes!" as Gant concluded.

They set to work feverishly, cutting down trees, whacking off the branches, lacing the logs together. They formed two rafts large enough to carry a wagon on each. Since Burnett was now riding at the head of the caravan with Gant, the Burnett wagon was the first to go over. This first trip nearly turned into a disaster. Peter Burnett had his twelve cows cowering on one raft as he poled. Perhaps it was a shift in current, perhaps one of the cows hiccoughed, but suddenly about twenty-five yards from shore the raft tipped and Peter Burnett found himself treading water with twelve cows mooing beside him. The soft brown eyes of the cows were stoic as ever as the creatures calmly swam toward the shore, prodded once or twice by a cursing, thrashing madman who swam among them waving his arms and swallowing his first gulps of Kansas River water.

The Burnett wagons finally crossed safely enough. The other wagons came on. Three small children nearly drowned but were saved by their mother . . . and spanked thoroughly before reaching the other shore. One wagon got loose from the ropes and rolled wildly back and forth on the flimsy raft while its owners pressed their weights against it from both sides to keep it aboard. However, at length the entire wagon train was reorganized on the far bank. Burnett turned to look back at the Kansas River and saw Papa standing at the river's edge. He did not seem to care about the turn of events; he looked as indifferent as ever.

Crossing the Kansas River had been a hardship but it had its moments of excitement and in retrospect became quite an important incident. From this point on, however, the trip consisted of molasses-thick mud which clung to the wagon wheels like a young babe to its mother. Above, the sky was clear and blue with no sign of clouds or rain. Underfoot, the ground was like a giant pot of mucilage. Progress slowed and spirits sagged.

By June the first, the party reached Black Warrior Creek, and here they held their monthly election for captain of the train. The quiet competence of Peter Hardeman Burnett had not gone unnoticed, and he was almost unanimously chosen as captain for the month of June. When he accepted the office, he rose to make a speech. He looked at the crowd of faces before him and changed his mind. He said, "All right, boys, let's get going!"

The covered wagons crawled along, across the east fork of the Blue River and then across the west fork, both swollen and whitecapped with rain. The night they made camp along the west fork a sudden drenching thunder-and-lightning storm crashed down to waken the sleeping pioneers. It drenched them all, blew down some five tents, and overturned four wagons. Many of the children were like little Sally Burnett, who clung to Harriet and whimpered, "Mommy, let's go back to where it's civilized."

Many years later Peter Burnett wrote that Harriet answered at this point in her gentle voice, "From now on, darling child, we have to make our own civilization and someday we'll be proud of it."

Storms, mud, accidents, mishaps, discomfort, fatigue . . . all made up the diversions of this trip, but on June 8 there appeared on the horizon the ultimate challenge. Indians! Harriett Burnett could see them plainly. There were close to a hundred of the Kansas and Osage tribes, drenched in red war paint that gleamed in the sun like blood. No sooner were they seen on the horizon than, screaming and yipping, they galloped their horses hellbent toward the wagon train.

There was no time to form a defense. Burnett had commanded "Halt!" the moment he had seen the Indians. There was no need to give that command. Each wagon stood motionless, its occupants stricken statuelike. Every eye was fixed in fascinated disbelief on the horde thundering down upon them.

Guns were out and at shoulder when a hundred yards away the warriors came to a simultaneous halt.

"Oh, God," one woman cried, "I see a scalp on the leader's belt," and so quiet were the other wagons that she could be heard everywhere. She collapsed sobbing on her husband's shoulder.

It was Peter Burnett, train captain, who rode out to meet the marauders, shotgun in hand and an uneasy feeling down his back. He could think of no Indian words to say in any tribal language so he contented himself with shouting, "What do you want?"

The leader of the party caressed the scalp at his waist while making ugly grimaces. A young buck acting as interpreter spoke at length to him. The leader replied with great passion, pointing with covetous eyes first at Harriet Burnett then at several of the other nearby women, who shuddered under his gaze.

The interpreter translated his chief's words haltingly. "We are . . . proud . . . warriors . . . Osage, Kansas tribes. We hunting many days . . . white man frightened away buffalo . . . Indians are hungry." The interpreter said in a menacing tone, "Women . . . children . . . old people at Indian village very hungry. We want your women . . ."

"Our women!" Burnett exploded. He leveled his gun.

". . . to give us food. We go away. Nobody hurt."

It was trickery. Burnett sneered, pointing to the chief, "Nobody hurt! What about that scalp?"

The interpreter spoke to the young leader, then said, "Chief found dead Sioux killed by snake. Took scalp. Had to come back from hunting trip with something!"

Burnett became hysterical with laughter. He threw back his head and howled. His whole body shook, his horse shook. So great was his reaction that he could not control his explosion of mirth at this turn of events. Indeed the whole wagon train swelled with one enormous laugh of relief and felt that nervous lightness which comes after a tense emotional strain.

The Indians shifted from side to side and began to look embarrassed. Harriet later said they resembled foreign dignitaries at a tea party, who laugh in forced little gusts at things they do not understand.

"We can't let our red brethren starve," Burnett shouted. "Give them a bag of corn meal, a side of smoked bacon, and a bag of flour from the main supply. We are getting away cheap at that."

The Indians were satisfied and rode away.

Let it not be thought that this in any way reduced Burnett's vigilance. In this country it was known that Indians followed slow-moving columns of wagons for miles, observing how the wagon train was handled. If the train seemed carelessly guarded and inadequately defensible, a large Indian attack would inevitably result. In preparation for this—in case it should happen to them—Captain Gant several times had the wagon train drive the wagons in a circle with the heads of the oxen and horses in the center and the wheels of the wagons interlocked to form a defense.

The Burnetts were reminded vividly that Indians were about after Peter had exchanged watches two nights in a row with a Mr. John Hood. The nights had been extremely cold, despite the fact that it was now late spring, and it was necessary for those on guard at night to wrap themselves in blankets against the wet wind of the prairie. A happy providence looked after Burnett, for the morning after his watch had been taken by Hood, the latter was found dead with several arrows in him. His gun had not been discharged, indicating that he had been surprised. After this, vigilance was increased, but no further incident occurred. For all their watchfulness, they never did see Indians during this stage of the trip.

When they were one month and 250 miles away from Missouri, they crossed over into Nebraska. The cows were behaving, the daily routine of living on the road had become habitual, and the women boasted to each other about the hardness of their backsides from sitting on the bouncing wooden seats.

This part of the valley of the Platte River was so well stocked with buffalo they could look ahead and see literally thousands of the beasts wherever the eye roamed. One had only to go up to the creatures and shoot them. The buffalo meat was sweet to the taste and readily digestible. The women cleaned the skins and saved them for some future practical use. Sad to say, one of the children was accidentally shot by an inexperienced rifleman.

The Platte River was over a mile wide and running too high to ford. The current was red with mud. Here there was no unscrupulous boatman to extort money from them, and a way across had to be decided upon. Camping on the river bank for the night, they held a meeting and decided to improvise boats out of skins, using wood from the wagons as frames. Each raft was manned by six men with ten others swimming alongside pushing. A dozen more swam ahead of the raft tugging on a strong rope.

The crossing began on June 29 and took them six days. They could not stop for Independence Day but celebrated it up to their ears in water. However, on July 5 the last wagon was safe. In an exuberance of freedom, the two fiddlers among the travelers began to play; a few young men, and then all of them, began to dance with their wives or the young girls of the wagons. Their gaiety was infectious and that afternoon the river's edge was alive with bouncing, capering men, women, and children, exultant at being alive and at once more having overcome an obstacle.

The valley of the Platte River on this side turned out to be wide, bare, and utterly treeless. For a reason none of them could understand, it was called the "coast of Nebraska." There was little comfort in the barren land, and the stamina of their animals suffered from lack of forage. Men, women, and children walked as much as possible to spare their beasts. Still inexperienced in certain elements of trail living, the travelers, who were dependent on Mother Nature to provide trees and wood for fuel, found themselves without this basic commodity. In this valley there was not a twig to be found. They could not build fires, and their meals of the next four days were sad concoctions of cold mush.

It took them a week to reach Fort Laramie in Wyoming. On this trek they saw everywhere the rotting carcasses of cattle, the wrecks of wagons, and even smelled at times to the point of nausea the stench of decaying animal flesh. In this country a new danger arose from the change in the nature of the soil. This was alkali country, and they had to be careful of the drinking water. The only way to be sure a spring or pool was safe was to find one that swarmed with insects or other life. It was better to push insects aside than to drink from a water hole that might prove dangerous or fatal.

Another danger from alkali was that it cut and rotted the feet of the horses and oxen. Now Harriet and the other women found a use for the buffalo and antelope skins they had saved. They made hoof gloves for their animals out of the dried skins.

Midnight of July 13, about a day out of Fort Laramie, a terrific thunder storm stampeded the animals several miles in every direction. When the storm struck, a guard sang out, "Twelve o'clock and all's hell!" And the men went in all directions to find their animals. After an entire night of hunting them down, all the cattle were regained.

Fort Laramie was the milestone for which they had all been waiting. The fort was a strategic point in the center of the Sioux country. Not only a trading center for the American Fur Company but an army post as well, the fort was both a refuge and a scene of dramatic interest. It was a clearing-house where Indians, soldiers, traders, riverboatmen, scouts—just about everybody mixed. Here trade went on in buffalo robes, blankets, guns, materials, and alcohol. Here information was exchanged, and plans made for continuing. Here new supplies were bought. The prices of these supplies were appalling to the Burnetts as well as to the other travelers—coffee was a dollar and a half a pound, brown sugar the same, flour twenty-five cents a pound, calico a dollar a yard.

One of the most important things about Fort Laramie was that members of the wagon train could take baths, wash their clothes, and sleep around the clock. Every member of the train registered at the fort. In this way the army kept some track of those passing through the country.

After two days in Laramie, the wagons took to the trail once again. Not a day's journey out but they found evidence of discarded paraphernalia of other trains, discarded articles of furniture, and messages written on the skulls of dead animals. Buffalo and antelope were scarce. They were made even more so by an English member of the party named Captain John Stewart. Captain Stewart enjoyed shooting for pleasure and was thereby blamed for flushing out the buffalo and antelope herds for miles around.

About a week out, Peter Burnett sighted a newly made grave. Fear once again gripped the party. Did it mean Indians? An epidemic? Peter Burnett read the inscription on the wooden cross, and the word was passed back from wagon to wagon. The grave marker read: "Here lies Joel Hembrae, six years old, run over by a wagon June 8, 1843." Joel's demise supplied an object lesson for Harriet, who would say to her boys when they misbehaved, "You know what happened to Joel Hembrae. He didn't mind his maw."

By the end of July they had left the Platte behind, and pushed up the Sweetwater River. Peter had carved the children's names on Independence Rock, and they had their first glimpse of the Rockies in the distance. Peter Burnett wrote later of this view of the Rockies, "At last we came in view of the eternal snows of the Rocky Mountains so we wound up the line two hours earlier than usual. Our hunters had brought in some fine antelope and two fat young buffalo. We had a feast. Campfire streaming up from the plain flooded the tents with mellow light and made the tops of the quadrangle barricade of wagons look like a fortification of molten gold. It was a beautiful evening. Bright stars in a blue vault, not a breath of air. Jim Wayne fiddled and we danced set after set on the sward. . . ."

They finally crossed the Continental Divide. Here the land was green, well watered and wooded. They caught trout in the streams. And so it went until they reached Fort Hall at the end of August. They rested for only a day and then pushed west across the barren sagebrush of Idaho to Fort Boise. It was September the first when they saw their first snow and descended into the welcoming valley of the Umatilla, which you can locate now on the borderline between the states of

Washington and Oregon. From here they proceeded to Whitman's Mission on the Walla Walla River. The Walla Walla would take them into the Columbia River. Rafts and boats were built to take them downstream. Their plan was to reach Fort Vancouver, the fur metropolis of the Oregon Territory, on what is now the Washington bank of the Columbia River. There Peter planned to hang out his lawyer's shingle.

Down the Columbia River they passed traders and loggers. Heavy rains and occasional rafts of logs, as well as tricky rapids, slowed their progress, but at last they reached their goal. At Vancouver a British ship lay at anchor waiting for a cargo of furs. As the Burnetts passed under the ship's rail on their raft, a sailor threw apples to the children. Unfortunately they missed all of them by about three inches. The plop of those apples in the water gave them perhaps one of the unhappiest moments of the journey since none of the Burnetts had eaten fresh fruit for many weeks.

They were at their goal. They had reached Oregon. But there was no celebration. Weariness provided a resigned acceptance. Now they must set to work. They had to find a temporary home, or build one, and meet the everyday challenge for subsistence.

EPILOGUE

The Burnetts settled in Vancouver and worked the land. Peter did hang out his shingle but more for prestige value than anything else since there were no courts. For five years they concentrated on solving the problems of making a comfortable home and raising healthy children. Recalling those years, Peter Burnett said, "It was a fine population; honest, because there was nothing to steal. Sober, because there was no liquor worth drinking. There were no misers because there was no money to hoard and everybody was industrious because it was work or starve."

This did not end the travels of the Burnetts. In July, 1848, when word surged across the High Sierras that gold had been found in California, Peter Burnett organized a company of 150 strong men and went off to find it. He promised his Harriet that he would either find gold in six months or return to settle down in Oregon for good.

Burnett was a man destined by history to be a leader and pioneer in the most exciting period of Western development. That same destiny kept him safe from all manner of disaster and personal sorrow. He safely followed the trail through the wild Sierra Nevadas that spelled death for so many. He met nothing worse than routine hardship. When he arrived at the gold fields, he panned with moderate success. This did not satisfy him, and, when he heard that John A. Sutter, Jr., was planning a real estate development in the Sacramento Valley, he joined in the land exploitation. He was very successful and by the spring of 1849, his whole family had joined him and set up housekeeping in Sacramento.

The legislature set up for the California Territory was in confusion. Accepted for statehood but not yet officially part of the Union, there was no due process of law and California had no state constitution.

Burnett felt a challenge in the need for a constitutional framework for the state. On September 13, 1849, he stood before a convention and named himself candidate for governor. He became the first governor of the State of California.

In August, 1878, this elder statesman and his beloved Harriet celebrated their golden wedding anniversary. Burnett made a speech: "Of all the wonderful things the West has meant to me, the most precious has been the continued good health of my dear wife. Thirty-five years ago we were not sure she would be with us six months. Thank God for keeping her well and leading us to this blessed land."

Big foot Wallace

There is, I am told, more mink of the finest quality in Texas than any place in the world. There are, I hear, more air-conditioned Cadillacs and more privately owned twin-engined planes in Texas than any place in the world. There are, I know, some of the finest orchestras and theatrical groups in the world in Texas. Maybe Texans are right about Texas after all.

YOU DON'T have to cross Texas personally to grant its size, but anyone who has lived there knows how much the vast distances influence the way he thinks. This has given rise to an accusation from other parts of the United States that the Texans are braggarts. Not so. They are merely reflecting their environment. When a Texan has the biggest, the greatest of one thing or another, he is being literal. People from Rhode Island, or Illinois, or New York, or even California can hardly contest it although they may resent it.

Being a Texan is actually a state of mind. You don't have to be born there to acquire it, or even raised there. Merely getting involved in its history is enough. And so it was with Bigfoot Wallace; never did Texas have a more militant and articulate champion than he.

Bigfoot Wallace was born in Virginia, but he became a real part of the early history of Texas. His name, given at birth, was William A. Wallace. In 1836, when he was nineteen years of age, he stood six feet two in his stocking feet. When he heard that his older brother and a cousin had eaten Mexican lead at Goliad, he borrowed money for his passage, picked up his rifle, and wrote "G.T.T." on the threshold of his father's house—Gone To Texas.

Back in the States those initials were a standing joke. They signified the hasty retreat of absconders, murderers, and sneak thieves to a haven beyond the long arm of the law. To young Wallace, however, they stood for bloody vengeance of his slaughtered kinfolk. And for Texas they meant the arrival on Texan soil of the man who was destined to become her own personal hero, who typified for all Texans, and for Americans in general, the men of Texas and everything they fought and died for.

The massacre of Goliad where the Wallace men died was fought fourteen days after the fall of the Alamo. The Mexican general, Urrea, caught over three hundred Texans in a trap near the town of Goliad. When the scrappy little Texan band had finally been subdued—which took General Urrea's army of one thousand a considerable amount of time and effort— the surviving Texans were marched into Goliad jail. A week later, on Palm Sunday, the general handed them over to his firing squads.

Twenty-seven men escaped and spread the news of the Goliad massacre through all the Texas settlements. The bitterness between the "Texians" and Mexicans had been fanned high by the Battle of the Alamo. Goliad doubled the heat of the blaze. It brought the wrath of Texas down upon Mexico's head. It also brought the youngest Wallace on the double all the way from Lexington, Virginia, to Galveston, Texas.

Big Billy arrived a little late for the battle of San Jacinto, the fight that brought the war to an end. During the next several decades, however, he more than made up for it by getting himself thoroughly involved in Lone Star history. In 1842, in an attempt to recapture Texas for Mexico, General Adrian Woll marched north and raided San Antonio. Some two hundred Texans, Wallace among them, waited for Woll just outside the city on the banks of Salado Creek. Woll was foolish enough to attack.

During the ensuing slaughter of Mexican troopers, General Matthew Caldwell, who was in command of the Texans, observed Billy Wallace shooting down foe after foe, cursing disappointedly after every shot. The general was about to investigate this strange behavior, when he saw Billy rush forward toward the Mexican lines with an exultant shout.

"Finally shot me one my size!" Wallace shouted, triumphantly flourishing his trophy in Caldwell's face. His trophy? A pair of Mexican trousers!

Later Sam Houston sent an avenging army under General A. Somervell after the retreating Woll just to teach Mexico a lesson. Wallace went along, of course. When Somervell ordered the disbanding of the expedition, about three hundred Rangers elected to stay and capture the Mexican town of Mier. They marched dismounted into the town, Wallace at the head, to engage an army of a thousand men under General Pedro d'Ampudia. The Mexicans were waiting for them. The first shot killed a friend of Wallace's just behind him. Immediately, a horde of Mexicans poured forth from the houses on either side. Wallace and his men whipped out their Bowie knives and after a bitter hand-to-hand fight left a mound of some twenty enemy dead over the body of their fallen comrade.

For forty-eight hours, the foolhardy Texans charged the Mexican artillery, fighting from house to house, chopping Ampudia's force down to less than four hundred. Luckily for the general, eight hundred Mexican reinforcements arrived. The remaining Texans were forced to surrender.

Along with his fellow prisoners, Wallace walked for two hundred miles in chains. The route led through Monterrey and Saltillo where they were exhibited to the hooting, filth-flinging populaces. Finally, they rested behind the walls of the Salado prison. Three days later, Wallace and 192 others made a wild break for freedom. Halfway to the border, after five waterless days under the broiling Mexican sun, they stumbled toward what they thought was a mirage. It turned out to be a real enough pool of water, but just as real were the Mexicans who sat there on their horses waiting for them.

Back in Salado, the Mexican commander ordered the 176 survivors to draw lots. Seventeen black beans and 159 white beans were put into a jar and each man drew blindfolded. Wallace said later that he grabbed two beans and picked the smaller one because he thought the black ones were somewhat larger. Legend has it that he offered to exchange his white bean for one of the black, but he denied this, insisting that at the moment of the drawing he felt he had but one life to lay down for Wallace.

The unfortunate holders of the black beans were shot, and the rest of the Texans were put to work building roads. Eventually Wallace was released, and made his way to New Orleans where he joined the police force just to get a fresh suit of clothes. He returned to Texas in time to rejoin the Rangers and march back into Mexico under General Zachary Taylor. He had the pleasure of receiving a white flag of surrender from the same soldier who had held the bean bowl at Salado and rode in triumph along the very roads he had helped to build as a prisoner.

According to some sources, Wallace got his nickname while a prisoner in Mexico City. None of the Mexican shoemakers had anything in stock that could fit the big man. Finally, special lasts had to be made to his measurement, and the name Bigfoot stuck with him for the rest of his life.

Think of a man over six feet tall, most of whose length is taken up by two incredibly long, incredibly slim, slightly bowed legs. Where his waist should be is a broad leather belt. Where his hips should be hang two holstered six guns. He wears skintight pants tucked into the tops of high-heeled boots with needle-point toes. On his head is an outlandish hat, with a crown that seems to brush the clouds and a rolled-up brim that could hold the Rio Grande at flood level.

Think of the way this man walks on the outside of his

arches. His hands swing casually but brushing lightly against the gun butts. His torso is relaxed and slouching. His steel-gray eyes stare out of an alert, weather-beaten face, the grim line of his mouth twitches quizzically at the corners.

Bigfoot never married, but he came close to it at least twice. The first time was just a year or two after he'd settled down in Texas. He was working alternately as a hunter and wood chopper. Both jobs paid well and both were equally hazardous. The Comanche and Lipan warriors didn't much care whether the man whose scalp they lifted toted an axe or a gun.

Naturally, the success of both these jobs depended on the individual's success in fighting off Indians. Bigfoot made out extremely well, better than anyone else, but he preferred hunting to wood chopping. The latter, he complained, required too many tools to suit his simple, one-track tastes.

"You can't chop down a tree with a rifle an' you can't shoot Indians with an axe an' you never know what you're goin' to be doin' next."

So, Wallace stuck to hunting. When he'd saved up the awesome sum of six hundred dollars, he wooed and won the hand of a young woman of Austin who promised to wait while he went off on one last hunting expedition. Unfortunately Bigfoot came down with a strong dose of typhoid, and by the time he recovered he'd lost all his hair. Being a little shy about facing his fiancée looking like a Comanche's idea of the Fourth of July, he hid out in the wilderness and rubbed bear grease into his scalp until the hair grew back in. But by that time his girl had met and married some other affluent member of the community, and Bigfoot was out of luck.

Bigfoot never went gunning for matrimony again, but the second chance came looking for him. During a brush with the Lipans, he was captured and taken along to their camp. The braves had a healthy respect for Wallace—he was famous among them as a courageous enemy—and they prepared to treat him accordingly. After a proper council, the tribe decided that Bigfoot was worth an hour or two of pleasant entertainment and pressed him into service as the main and only event on the program. His role was a simple one. All he had to do was stand tied to a stake surrounded by burning brush.

Just as the torch was to be applied, a squaw burst through the council ring, her head covered as a sign of mourning. She had come to protest the burning of the white warrior. It seems he had been responsible for her husband's death. She therefore demanded that, according to tribal law, he be awarded to her as a replacement.

At first Wallace was highly pleased by the interruption. For some reason not yet clear to him, the burning had been called off, and he was being handed over to a squaw who was at least young and not unattractive.

But when he learned of the terms of his rescue, Wallace shook her loose, walked back to the stake and, resuming his place, said to the braves, "Come on, light your fire!"

The Lipans, amazed at such courage and strength of will, awarded him instead to an old squaw who had lost a son. Wallace was taken into the tepee as an adopted son, learned the Lipan tongue, and eventually managed to escape and make his way back to his *compadres.*

Did a member of the fair sex come into view, this man was the model of chivalry. However, on Saturday nights when he rode into town on a black horse, the scalps of his enemies decorated his saddle, and tied behind was a gallon of whiskey to wash the trail dust out of his throat before he started the evening's drinking. The first thing he did on arriving in town was to stand in the middle of Main Street and declare himself ready, willing, and able to take on any fifty men, so long as they didn't hail from his part of the country. He bragged about toting a longhorn under each arm. Swore he'd rather ride a bolt of greased lightning through a cactus thicket for amusement than spark a girl. Fellow Texans loved it—non-Texans weren't amused.

216

After the Mexican War had ended, Wallace settled down on a ranch on the Medina River, where he became famous as the man who protected and helped his neighbors. In one year he killed 150 panthers, to the great delight of the settlers whose stock had suffered severe losses until Wallace came along. No score was ever kept of the number of times he rode to the rescue of some beleaguered family standing off a marauding bunch of Comanches. Fights with Indians were too common to mention. But those panthers now, they were something to talk about!

Think of this man, this seemingly impossible character, and see in him something of that old "Kaintuck," Davy Crockett, and James Bowie and Jack Hayes of the Rangers—the hunters, soldiers of fortune, frontiersmen, settlers, the whole kit and kaboodle who left the plantation-rich South and the valleys of the Ohio and Mississippi for a dusty, canyoned, cactus-grown, Comanche-infested region where farming and ranching were carried out with one hand on the plow and the other on the rifle. Think of this man, and see behind him the dim shapes of the coonskin cap and the Bowie knife, the emigrants' wagon and the long-horned cattle bawling their way up the Chisholm Trail. And as the figures waver and fade around his long, thin frame, watch as they come together and merge into one dominant image, the towering stature of Bigfoot Wallace.

Wallace stood the sedentary life as long as he could, but when a stage line started to operate between San Antonio and El Paso, he joined up as escort and driver. For more than twelve years, he took the mail over six hundred miles of Apache-infested country and learned more about the Apaches than any man alive.

Once when his mules were stolen during a rest period at a spring, he left the other guards to watch the coach while he walked eighty miles to El Paso for a fresh team. He drove that coach until the Civil War put it out of business, and then went back to his ranch.

Most of his neighbors who were fit and able joined the Confederate forces, but Wallace refused to have any part of that war. He believed, as did Sam Houston, that secession was an unwise move, but at the same time he couldn't bear the thought of fighting against the land of his birth, Virginia. When the war ended, and the Federal Army along with the Texas Rangers went on making Texas safer and safer, Bigfoot decided to take a holiday and go back to the Old Dominion for a visit.

Actually, he was a peaceable enough citizen—within the limits of his own Texas township or country. The moment he passed over the state line he became all "hoss and alligator with a touch of the snapping turtle thrown in!" In Texas he sang of love—on a foreign strand all he could remember were salty ballads about rip-roarin', bar-smashin', town-pulverizin' cowboys. In Texas on Sundays, he was as good a Baptist as the other *compadres* over whom the women had sweated since the day of their births. Yet, strangely enough, when he arrived in parts where he was unknown, he suddenly began to invoke some outlandish private deity with his "Ah-ha, San'ntone!" It was a difficult trip for him—and for everyone he met.

He bought an outfit of clothes he thought would go well back in civilization, but the frock coat split up the back the first time he tried it on, and the shoes pinched his feet unmercifully. When he finally did leave on the Indianola stage for the Gulf steamer that took him to New Orleans, he wore his usual buckskins and carried a pair of derringers and "Old Butch," his scalping knife.

If this towering, buckskin-clad frontiersman, with his long hair and rough-spoken ways, looked strange to Eastern eyes, imagine how the States looked to him! In New Orleans he put up at a hotel that had hundreds of rooms and mile after mile of corridor. And the whole building was lit by brass knobs that burned gas! What with the lack of a map and the extreme danger of fire, Bigfoot hired a bellboy to sleep outside his room and guide him down to the dining room each morning.

During his stay in New Orleans, he attended a quadroon ball, where he sampled strange drinks concocted of many different kinds of fiery waters, and was surrounded by a bevy of masked ladies. Before he left the festivities, he taught them a dance called the "Stampede," which he said was popular back in Texas.

According to his directions, "the ladies range themselves on one side of the room and the gentlemen on the other. Then one of the gentlemen neighs and if a lady whinnies in answer, they both step forward and become partners for the dance. If the gentleman is very homely and after neighing three times no lady should answer, he steps out of the ring and hopes for better luck next time.

"When the couples are all paired off in this way, the manager calls out 'Gallopade all' and all 'lope around the room briskly three or four times. Then the gentlemen 'curvet' to their partners and the ladies coquettishly back their rears and kick up at the gentlemen. Then the ladies canter up to the gentlemen who rear and plunge for a while, then seize the ladies' hands and pace gracefully off in couples around the room. The first couple then wheels and goes off at a two-forty lick, second couple ditto, and so on until the race becomes general, when the manager calls out 'Whoa!' and everybody comes to a sudden halt. The manager then calls out 'Walk your partners'; 'pace your partners'; 'trot your partners'; and 'gallopade all' again, faster and faster until the 'sprained' and 'wind-galled' and 'shot stock' begin to 'cave in' when he calls out 'Boo!' and throws his hat into the ring! A general 'stampede' follows; the gentlemen neigh, curvet, and pitch; the ladies whinny, prance, and kick, chairs and tables are knocked over, lights blown out, and everybody tumbles over everybody else till the whole set is piled up in the middle of the room; and so the dance ends."

He explained to the city folk not to attempt this dance until it was time to go home for "generally, things were smashed up after the 'Stampede' and it would be hard to get the ball going again."

Wallace swore the quadroon ball actually attempted the Stampede and went right along with his instructions until the stampede itself. It ended in a magnificent knock-down, drag-out brawl, in which Wallace enjoyed himself thoroughly.

Back in Virginia, Wallace was received enthusiastically by his family and his old friends, but it soon became clear to him that they regarded him as a half-civilized savage. He tried to correct the impression, but the crowd seemed more disposed to accept his tall tales as the truth than the truth itself. He decided to play up to their expectations. He told them about the spider in Texas as big as a peck measure, whose bite can only be cured by music. He described, to the shivering delight of the young Virginian belles, the "Santa Fe," a monster with a hundred legs with a sting in each one and fangs as big as a rattlesnake's. The biggest and the best brass band in the country couldn't cure the sting of the "Santa Fe."

He swore that all Texans had to wear tarantula boots made of alligator skin and centipede hunting shirts of rattlesnake hide, and chew tobacco and drink whiskey in order to stay alive. He explained this was why the Temperance Society never stood a chance along the Rio Grande.

They asked him about mirages. He told them about the one he saw of a buffalo herd that stampeded and kicked up so much dust it hid the sun for three days!

All in all, Wallace had a rare old time for himself back in his native Virginia. But he was never as happy as he was when he finally got back to Texas. At home he got into a fight with Indians as soon as possible and ate six pounds of buffalo hump, a side of ribs, and a marrow gut just to get to feeling human again.

The young boy who had left Virginia so many years before

had grown away from the East, the wealthy, settled East which was doing all it could to forget that it, too, had once been a frontier country. William A. Wallace, who left his father's house to return as Bigfoot Wallace, Indian hunter, veteran of the Mexican wars, Texas Ranger, stagecoach driver, and the best obstetrician along the Medina River, was a man from another planet as far as the East was concerned— an oddity. A hero to be sure, but nevertheless a curiosity to be gaped and wondered at, a relic of a past that persisted in keeping up the pretense of a reality that no longer existed.

And as for Bigfoot? Reality to him was his ramshackle "ranch" in dusty, drought-ridden Texas, along with the ranches of the German settlers and one-street towns of frame buildings, the roundups and the rustlers, and once in a while the Apache and the panther.

Before he died, Wallace lived to see the Texas he knew come closer and closer to the East he no longer understood or even wanted to understand. Yet, Texas never forgot him. They named a town after him, presented him with 125 acres as a gift, and gave him the rare experience of seeing himself cast in bronze.

In 1899 he died, in bed, at the age of eighty-two. He was buried in the state cemetery in Austin, and his epitaph reads:

BIGFOOT WALLACE

Here Lies He Who Spent His

Manhood Defending the Homes

of

Texas

Brave Honest and Faithful

Born April 13, 1817

Died Jan. 7, 1899

Think of Bigfoot the next time you run across a strutting, boasting, son of the Lone Star. Think of Bigfoot when you hear the drawl and the hearty way of talking. That's Bigfoot talking, son. Ah-ha, San'ntone!

The Man Who Started it All and the Man Who Couldn't Forget

A man who has wealth feels a great desire for an accompanying grace called glory. Men who have glory and not wealth just as keenly desire the thing they lack. And so rich men bask in the glory of famous men, and famous men sup and break bread with the men who have wealth. This is the story of two men who should have had both fabulous wealth and undying glory— and got neither.

THE DREAM of many Europeans coming to America was to found a feudal barony of a European order. The Spanish were successful in doing this for a while before the United States opened many of their tracts of land for settlement. A Swiss adventurer, John August Sutter, came to the Sacramento Valley to do just this on an immense tract of land he had secured from the Spanish governor, Alvarado.

On arriving in the Sacramento Valley, which was the center of his grant, Sutter established a fort which he named New Helvetia. He set to work developing his property with the aid of Indians, Kanakas, Mexicans, and Americans, who would labor for food, shelter, and small wages.

New Helvetia grew steadily. The only excitement that stopped the daily routine of work was in 1844, when Frémont and his company stumbled down the western slope of the Sierras more dead than alive from exposure and starvation. Sutter sheltered them, doctored them back to health, and sent them on.

As his enterprises developed and New Helvetia grew in population, Sutter decided to build a sawmill on the south fork of the American River. He enlisted a partner, James W. Mar-

225

shall, in the venture. The plan was for the two men to process the lumber and share equally in the profits.

Work on the sawmill was almost completed by January of 1848. Holding up completion was the tailrace, which was found to be too shallow. Marshall tried to deepen it by flooding water through it each night. On the morning of January 24, after damming off the flowing water, he stepped down into the ditch to see what progress had been made.

There was something shiny on the bedrock under the still water.

It looked like gold!

Marshall picked up a nugget and took it to the camp housekeeper, Mrs. Elizabeth Wimmer. She had a kettle of lye on the stove for soap making, and she popped the nugget into the boiling liquid. She cooked the shiny metal all day. When Marshall returned that night and found that it had not tarnished, he was sure that he had found gold.

Like a man pursued by devils, he hurried to his partner at the fort. Here the two men made further tests. The results convinced them. It was definitely gold! They solemnly swore to each other to keep it a secret.

Soon, however, it leaked out, and word got around that there was GOLD in the American River! By summer of 1849, the California Gold Rush was in full swing. From the Eastern cities of the United States, from Great Britain and Europe and Asia, men crowded into California-bound ships with dreams of great fortunes. The established California towns such as San Jose, San Francisco, and Monterey were emptied of all men who could walk, ride, or crawl. Settlers who had barely established themselves on the western side of the Mississippi streamed across the Sierras. A writer of the day, Walter Colton, wrote home, "Such a mixed and motley crowd, such a restless, roving, rummaging, ragged multitude I have never seen."

Sutter was inundated. He was overwhelmed by the thousands and thousands of squatters who plunked themselves down on the huge acreage given to him by the Spanish. It was his property, he protested. He appealed to the United States Congress to help him maintain it. He received no assistance: California was now United States territory and soon to be a state; the land after all had been injudiciously given away by a now-foreign power. The self-styled Baron of the Sacramento found himself in a one-sided fight for his alleged rights against a government sworn to a policy of homesteading for expansion.

Sutter died, an old man, preparing yet another futile petition of his rights for consideration in Washington.

James W. Marshall, the actual discoverer of the precious metal, died a forgotten and embittered man. It was his discovery, and he had received neither wealth nor credit. It was the indifference, the exclusion from glory, that hurt him. He finally went so far as to have cards printed which featured a drawing of Sutter's Mill and a handwritten autograph of: JAMES W. MARSHALL, *The Discoverer of Gold, January 24, 1848,* which he handed out to all who would accept them.

Of Gold and Men

Sometimes I can stand in a place and sense that a mystery is near. Many times I've had this feeling. The first time I gazed upon Superstition Mountain I felt strange vibrations. Many years later, I learned of the mysterious happenings about which I invite you to read.

THERE IS much in common between the men who go down to the sea in ships and the men who go down into the mines with picks. This was particularly true when men sailed before the mast and when the early miners had to face the challenge of rock, sand, vegetation, and the vagaries of nature. Yet both these pursuits have called to men from times past.

Motivated by boredom, adventure, curiosity, or lust for wealth, men have traveled, seeking the lands of easy riches. The experiences fate meted out were varied: some men died before arriving at their goal; some became farmers or storekeepers or real estate dealers; some found gold or silver or copper; many met violent deaths with heads split open or bullets between their shoulder blades. Many lived to continue their unavailing search until old age defeated them.

Wherever a land has riches in the ground, there you will find stories about the men who found them, fought over them, and developed them. In the United States, California, Nevada, Arizona, and Montana contained our richest gold, silver, and copper mines. Some of these mines became the basis of enormous fortunes and created American financial dynasties. Some of the mines function today, many have been abandoned, and some are lost, their location shrouded in mystery.

There is something to intrigue the imagination in the mine that is lost, its riches hidden and waiting to be refound. Take, for example, the Lost Dutchman Mine of Phoenix, Arizona. The story of this mine began in 1830, in the state of Sonora, which is the part of Mexico closest to the Arizona border. The leading characters in the story were Don Miguel Peralta, a wealthy cattle rancher; Rosita, his beautiful daughter; and Carlos, her suitor. Carlos was not the choice of Don Miguel, and, when Don Miguel learned that the young lovers planned to marry, Carlos was forced to flee. There are many "accidents" on these rancheros at the hands of the great dons turned *vaqueros,* and flight was considered the course of wisdom.

Fast on his feet when circumstances warranted it, Carlos escaped to the north. However, the infuriated father was not to be eluded and sent two Yaqui Indian scouts after him. They found the runaway camped on the slopes of Superstition Mountain in sight of what is now Phoenix, Arizona. Then, as now, strangely dark and forbidding, this mountain peak raised its barren head in the midst of bright desert hues and sunshine. The Indians brought Carlos back to Sonora and into Don Miguel's presence. Here the young man, his bonds loosened, arrogantly threw a handful of enormous gold nuggets at the feet of his captor.

No doubt the gold spoke a language Don Miguel understood, for he immediately forgave the lovers and blessed their marriage . . . and organized an expedition to the north. The mine which Carlos had found was on the highest peak of Superstition Mountain. This peak is shaped like the crown of a Mexican hat, so Don Miguel named it *La Mina Sombrero.* To this mine Don Miguel was content to send small yearly expeditions to take out limited amounts of gold. However, when the United States acquired the Arizona Territory in 1848, the Mexican decided to throw caution to the winds and take out all that he could. He feared, and with good cause, that his treasure would be claimed as American property, and he sent a party of three hundred men and six hundred pack animals to bring out his fortune.

Now, in planning this expedition, Don Miguel failed to take into consideration that most dangerous and bloodthirsty of all the Southwestern Indian tribes, the Apaches. To send such a large caravan into Arizona territory was to attract Indian attention immediately. To send them comparatively unarmed was to issue a gilt-edged invitation to slaughter. Of the three hundred men, only two small boys escaped massacre by lying still and pretending to be dead. After the carnage was over, they made their painful way back to Sonora with the tragic news.

At this point the story of the mine disappears for about thirty years. Presumably Rosita and her Carlos were allowed to marry and live happily ever after, for nothing more is heard of them.

By 1870, settlers moved into the Phoenix area. Among them was a Dutchman named Jacob Walz. Walz may have been a native of Germany rather than the Netherlands; it was common practice to refer to German immigrants as *deutsch-man* which was automatically shortened to Dutchman. Whatever Walz's antecedents, he had an adventurous nature and spent much time exploring the country around Phoenix, and even went up into Superstition Mountain. On one such trip, he lost his way and before long ran out of food and, more importantly, water. Suffering acutely from heat and thirst, he stumbled onto a recently made trail, which led him into the camp of three middle-aged Mexicans. They received him kindly and gave him food and water.

When he had regained his strength, he became curious and asked, "Why are you three camping up here on the mountain?"

"*Por el oro*, signor. For gold!"

Walz did not show any emotion, although his heart must have leaped. "What gold?"

"*La Mina Sombrero!*" they replied in unison. They told him their story. Two of the three men were the boys who had escaped the Apache massacre thirty years before. It had taken them these thirty years to gather the equipment, and the courage, to return and rework the mine. In proof of what they said they showed old Walz bags of gold nuggets.

They made the further mistake of describing to him where the mine was. This was as good as signing their death warrant, for Walz repaid their hospitality by grabbing his rifle and shooting all three men as they sat around their own campfire. He dragged their bodies to a crevice and piled rocks on them.

There was no one to protest when Walz claimed the mine for his own. He lived in Phoenix, from which he would disappear periodically to come back with great bags of gold nuggets. He boasted of his bonanza and many a spy was set to watch him, but none were ever able to follow him to the mine. He never shared his secret and is known to have killed eight men, including his own nephew, for trying to trail him. He was the most feared of all the fearsome characters on the Arizona scene at the time.

Men never caught up with Walz but death finally did. When he lay wracked with pneumonia and old age, he called on the only man who had ever befriended him, Dick Holmes. To him he said, "You shall have the gold. I have covered the mine with rocks and logs and planted a cactus on the spot. Look under my bed. In that metal box is a map and some nuggets. You can read the map if you know the key. The key is a paloverde tree with a pointing arm. It's located not far from The Hat, the highest peak." He told Holmes more, including details of the original murders . . . and died in the middle of his recital. Dick Holmes, who seems to have been a sober kind of man, found the metal box. It contained the map and the nuggets as promised, but Dick Holmes did not find the mine. Although he searched all the remainder of his life for the paloverde tree with the pointing arm, he never found it.

When Dick Holmes died, his son, Brown Holmes, inherited

the story, the legacy of the map, and the gold nuggets. At this writing, he and his sons are still searching. They still live in hope of locating the Lost Dutchman Mine. They are not alone in their search, for many have tried and none have succeeded in finding it.

Superstition Mountain has brought tragedy to the lives of the many who have come to find its treasure. The story of the lost mine is known, and thousands have arrived hopefully at the foot of Superstition Mountain. The mere sight of the threatening peaks turns many away but hundreds have roamed the craggy rocks, digging, prodding, searching. None have found gold, several have lost their lives.

One of the most chilling occurrences was the adventure of Adolph Ruth, who, in 1930, went alone on Superstition Mountain. He never came out. A sheriff's posse and others searched for two months and failed to find him. The following winter an archeological expedition found his bleached skull with a bullet hole in the temple. Half a mile away they found the bones of his headless torso and the remains of his camp with all its personal effects intact. It was learned that one thing was gone from the camp: a map which had been acquired from the descendants of the Peralta family in Mexico. Who shot and dismembered Adolph Ruth? How close he came to finding the Lost Dutchman, or whether there is another who now has the secret, nobody can say.

There is other evidence of a presence on Superstition Mountain. As recently as 1946, a New Yorker named Mayer Schuelebtz disappeared on the mountain. Sheriff James Heron and a posse rode up to search for him. "Somebody" fired at them across one of the deep canyons and forced them to take cover. Schuelebtz was found wandering about a few days later, suffering considerably from exposure. His story of being shot at and getting lost did not clear up the mystery.

An ex-Marine, Davis O'Hara of Milwaukee, was lost on Superstition and wandered two days before stumbling back to his own camp. He found his tent and supplies completely destroyed. By whom and why are unanswerable questions.

And so the mystery stands. Will there ever be one lucky enough to surmount this history of failure, find the mine and, despite taxes, live as did Croesus of old?

Captain Samuel Samuels

A ship under full sail is to me a very beautiful thing.
She is alive and breathing, and I am never surprised
to find myself almost talking to her as I walk her deck
or hold her wheel. The ships of the days of sail, those
incredibly beautiful vessels fitted together by master
craftsmen, made America mistress of the seas through
a good part of the nineteenth century. But, though
they were beautiful to the eye, life on them was hard
and brutal, and many are the stories told of tragic
happenings on them as they sailed the seas. The cap-
tains of these ships may have loved them as I do, but
they had little respect for the crews that manned
them. Now not all captains managed to maintain
discipline under difficult circumstances. Which is
why I admire this captain who did.

SAMUEL SAMUELS (nowhere does one find reference
to him as Sam) had an unhappy childhood. It would
seem that he had a stepmother who does credit to all
the horrid stepmothers of literature. And so, at the age of
eleven, resolving—with the decisiveness which was to charac-
terize him in emergencies thereafter—that there was not room
in the same home for them both, he ran away to sea. This
was in 1834, and it proved to be a wise move on his part. For
by 1854 he had become commander of the U.S. packet ship
Dreadnought. Captain Samuel Samuels sailed her between
New York and Liverpool for seventy-eight voyages.

Packet ships carried both freight and passengers, and the
various lines vied with each other to maintain regular sched-
ules in order to attract passengers. They also competed for
speed. The *Dreadnought,* under Captain Samuels, claimed

239

remarkable speeds. There is some agreement among historians that Captain Samuels, in common with other skippers, was sometimes a little overenthusiastic in logging sporadic speeds accomplished by his vessel (who can question the speed logged at sea), but the fact remains that the *Dreadnought* made some very respectable runs. One of her best was from the coast of England to New York in nineteen days!

Now a first-rate skipper is not made in a minute. Between the time eleven-year-old Samuel decamped from home and the day he stood on the bridge of the *Dreadnought,* most of the traditional misadventures of a seafarer's life befell him. Early in his career, young Samuel made a "Shanghai passage." Because life on merchant ships was hard, the masters often brutal, and wages ashore relatively high, it was difficult to fill a ship's complement. With sailing time near and berths unfilled, crimps scoured the water-front dives and streets to shanghai the rest of the needed hands. In this manner, young Samuel was kidnapped and woke up one day to find himself in the hands of a ship's captain who, having paid his crimps eighty dollars apiece for each member of his reluctant crew, was determined to get it back from them in sweat and work, bloodily if necessary. Young Samuels had a bad time of it, but he came through.

We are indebted for these details to Captain Samuels himself, who, in the days of his retirement, re-evoked the gusty adventurousness of the sea by writing his memoirs. From his own description, he emerges as a kind of nineteenth-century Superman, equal to every occasion even though unaided by space guns or X-ray eyes.

Once he narrowly escaped a second shanghaiing in New Orleans. On this occasion—with more business acumen than ethics—the crimps had included a corpse, recently dead of yellow fever, whom they carried aboard as though he were merely drunk. Presumably the thought of the captain's fury when he discovered the trick spurred Samuel to desperate action. He slipped overboard and swam for the docks before the vessel sailed.

He has recounted in his memoirs a period of service in the Texan Navy. He also tells us that he shipped as a mate in the *Caledonia,* a British ship whose master wanted a two-fisted Yankee to share the voyage, one who was a "blower and a striker."

At any rate, he was a seasoned and experienced sailor when he became master of the *Dreadnought*—210 feet long, with a beam of 40 feet, a depth of 26, and a registered tonnage of 1,413 tons. Not quite a clipper ship, she was sharper-ended than the older packets.

Captain Samuels, like the other masters of these clipper sailing ships, had a true identification with his boats. It was more important to all of them to make a record and to sail their ships cleanly than it was to protect the lives of their expendable crew.

The *Dreadnought* sailed the seas for fifteen years till she was wrecked off Cape Horn in 1869. In that time, she made some wonderful crossings, probably because Captain Samuels sailed her as hard by night as by day, risky though this was because of the combined hazard of icebergs and the fatigue of his men.

The versatile Samuel—who like most captains of the time, was, when necessary aboard ship, doctor, lawyer, clergyman, navigator, merchant, and banker, as well as, in a pinch, cook, carpenter, sailmaker, and rigger—added on some occasions the talents of midwife to the list of his capacities. Indeed all of his own children were delivered by himself. He took great pride, too, in the fact that his was a well-run ship. Although his passengers did their own cooking, he supplied them with more than the ordinary staples of oatmeal and water common to similar passenger ships. He gave them a ration of salt beef, and he actually had a cowshed for fresh milk for babies.

It has been noted that Captain Samuels was also the doctor for his ship. What a nineteenth-century captain might do when confronted with the assortment of medicaments in the medicine chest, probably kept many an ailing sailor from reporting sick. There is a legend of a puzzled skipper who divided the medicine chest's contents and put them in individual bottles, labeled "A" and "B," for "Above" and "Below." Anyone reporting for medical attention was asked the location of his symptoms. If they were above the waist, he received the works from bottle A; if below, from bottle B. Today this would be considered pretty radical therapy, more likely to kill than cure the patient, but Captain Samuels was no less drastic in his treatment of himself when he came down with cholera on board ship in the 1859 epidemic. A lesser man would surely have died of his remedies, if not from the disease. However, Captain Samuels survived both. His treatment included a hot mustard bath, dosing with a mixture of brandy, cayenne pepper, laudanum and angostura bitters, and the application, as a climax, of a turpentine cloth over the entire abdomen!

One of his voyages above all others stays in the memory and evokes the picture of a real captain and a real man. It was a return voyage from Liverpool, and his crew of "packet rats" included several of a group that called itself "the Bloody Forties." These gentlemen had been questioned about the murder of a sea captain on a previous passage to Liverpool. Signing on to the *Dreadnought*, their greed and hostility to authority no wit lessened by the previous bloodletting, they decided among themselves to seize the ship and become pirates! Captain Samuels, in an enviably melodramatic literary style, recounts in his memoirs that the plot against him was hatched at a certain "Mother Riley's Den." Here it was decided "to give the skipper of the *Dreadnought* a swim."

On this particular passage, Captain Samuels's officers left something to be desired: the mate was an old man and the second a coward, says Captain Samuels in his memoirs. Furthermore Captain Samuels did not trust his steerage passengers; he suspected that some of them had come aboard to assist in the skulduggery intended by his crew. However, the good captain did not go looking for trouble; he was merely wary of his passengers. With his seamen he took more direct action.

As soon as the boat was out of sight of land, he ordered the crew forward and demanded they give up their knives to the ship's carpenter. Resistance was loud and belligerent. A lesser man than our worthy captain might have compromised but Captain Samuels informed his crew that their plot was known to him. There were some in the crew, he noted, who had sailed with him before. They knew, he declared, that the plotters would not get their way without a fight. There was much muttering, but he got the knives, his ship's carpenter broke the points, and the knives were returned to their owners. Having won his point, Captain Samuels declared that it upset him to see the men shivering, whether with cold or apprehension he did not know or care. He ordered grog all around and withdrew. This was Samuels at his best, the picture of an implacable master, but none the less one who was aware of the physical needs of his men.

Nevertheless, all was not well. The next morning, the crew was slow in carrying out his orders. A catastrophe was narrowly averted as the ship came about. Samuels bided his time. A few hours later the helmsman failed to reply "Aye, aye, sir" to an order. The captain, no man for arguing a point of authority, hauled off and let him have it.

He sent the man below and had him put in irons. The crew muttered, and, on his order to "Haul taut the weather mainbrace," did not obey.

Captain Samuels called them forward. They assembled, silent and sullen. He asked them only one question: "Why don't you obey orders?" They answered they would do so only after their shipmate who had been put in irons was released.

And now his memoirs picture him confronting his mutinous crew, alone and unafraid, a cutlass at his side and a brace of pistols in his hands. He writes—in quaintly high-flown language more often found in penny dreadfuls or shilling shockers than on the bridge of a ship at sea—of facing them down with vast courage and resolution. "Men," he tells the crew, "you have found your match." "Death," he adds, "to the first man who dares advance," and to one of them, "You cowardly dog, you shall bite the dust for this." Where the miscreant could have found enough dust to bite at sea is a question, but in any event the mutineers seemingly were not impressed, and showed no signs of yielding.

Captain Samuels went forward to deal with them. This failing, he then told them they should receive no food or water until they returned to duty. The crew jeered.

The men retreated to their quarters, and the captain found himself faced with the prospect of sailing his ship with only his inadequate officers and a few boys as crew.

The wind freshened. The royals, and later the topgallants, were furled. The topsails had to be left as they were, for there were too few hands to have hoisted them again. The ship rode out the storm, Captain Samuels himself standing at the helm for two days.

The storm must have been considered a test by the mutinous men. When the weather calmed, they realized that the captain had somehow done without them. However, they still refused duty. The captain himself, with only the third mate to help him, was forced to attend to the sails as the ship was put about.

At this point a number of the steerage passengers began to take sides with the mutineers. And Captain Samuels stepped, as it were, to the bar and became a lawyer. He warned the passengers that assisting the mutineers in any degree would make them accessories to the fact and liable to the same penalties. "But," he advised them, "it will not be necessary to wait for a maritime court to act on this. At sea, I am the Law." Anyone siding with the crew would be put in irons. And, to demonstrate that this was no idle threat, he did not bother to wait for such a move. He actually put one of them, who dared answer him, in irons. This action effectively discouraged the others.

Meanwhile fifty-six hours had passed since those in revolt had had anything to eat. Captain Samuels realized that he might well expect an attack on the galley. Choosing among the emigrant passengers chiefly those who had seen service in the German Army, he armed them with iron bars.

At this point two young friends of the crew tossed their knives overboard and begged to be allowed to rejoin the company. The whole idea had lost its fascination for them when the ringleader, seeking to relieve his frustrations by exerting his authority on his own small band, had "ill-temperedly" hit one of them with an iron belaying pin.

The expected attack on the galley occurred at eight bells. The passengers and Captain Samuels repelled the attack. One by one, the crew capitulated. Only the leader of the ineffectual mutiny, one Finnigan, refused to give in. The captain, understandably exasperated by a holdout, lost his temper. He hauled off and flattened Finnigan so that he measured his length along the deck.

All hands having apologized, except Finnigan, the loquacious captain delivered himself of an address which must have been sheer joy. He recorded it himself for posterity. "Now men," says Captain Samuels, "let it be understood that you are to jump when you are spoken to, and instead of walking, you are to run to obey the orders given! The last order I gave you, which you disobeyed, was 'Haul taut the weather mainbrace.' I now repeat it. 'Haul taut the weather mainbrace!' "

The erstwhile mutineers not only hauled taut the weather mainbrace, they jumped to it.

Coffee was then served all around to the hungry men, except for Finnigan. He would not summon the words for an apology, and so he was put in the sweatbox, in irons. A little of that sort of thing goes a long way, and inside a half-hour, Finnigan capitulated. He made a handsome apology and added that anyone who said the captain was a coward was a d----d liar.

Like many a man who turns to heaven when success attends him, Captain Samuels had "got religion" at the time he took command of the *Dreadnought*, and had forsworn the use of profanity. He therefore received Finnigan's apology with the dignified and uprighteous remark that he might leave out the word "d----d." "If anyone is going to swear on board this packet," he stated, "it is myself!"

Incredible as it seems, the voyage ended with good will on both sides. At its conclusion, Captain Samuels addressed his men most touchingly. He reviewed the early part of his forecastle life, recounting how, like they, he too had been preyed upon by those ashore, drugged, bought, and robbed.

"I begged my crew," wrote Captain Samuels later, "to break the chains that bound them to the depraved life they were leading, and assert the manhood God had given them for a better purpose than to be the slaves of boarding-house keepers and crimps." He ended his discourse on an elevated note of prayer which he says brought tears to the eyes of most of them. The captain, in fine form, declared by way of final valedictory, full of the magnanimity that brings out both the best and the oratorical in most of us, that he never expected to have a better set of sailors with him.

There is no mention in Samuels's account of how this touching scene ended. Were three rousing cheers given? We do not know, but we are made to understand that the crew said they would henceforth be pleased to ship out with him on any voyage whatsoever!

Of Silver and Men

*There is an old legend of a man who spent his whole life
searching for gold. He found it four times, then considered the trouble the precious metal would bring
him in the kind of life he would have to lead and the
kind of people he would have to associate with, and
decided that the real fun was looking for it. Always
he moved on to the next claim, and he died happy,
still searching.*

T HE discovery of silver in the United States was a world-
shattering event. It was found in such quantities that
it revolutionized the world's economic structure.

The mountains of Nevada are stark and terrible, winter-
bound and gale-swept six months of the year. Yet to the west-
ward-searching prospectors, these mountains beckoned, offering a great reward.

There were many prospectors for gold along the western
slopes of the Virginia Range in the autumn of 1859. One group
of men in particular were avoided by the others because of
their roughness, and the roughest of all were Peter Reilly and
Pat McLaughlin.

A region called the "Washoe" was credited at the time with
yielding enough gold to get a man drunk Saturday night and
sober him up Sunday morning. The big complaint was that
while traces of gold were to be found in the heavy blue clay
indigenous to the region, "the blue stuff" was difficult to work
and, for the time spent, gave relatively little gold.

Then Reilly and McLaughlin sent a specimen of the clay to
an assay office in California. Within a few months the Western
World knew that the despised blue stuff was silver in an un-
familiar geological form but of almost unbelievable richness.
The silver rush started.

The two prospectors staked their claim and were riding on top of the world when they were informed by a sanctimonious Nevadan named Comstock that they had jumped a claim to which he had an undisputed title! Reilly and McLaughlin, who were ignorant men, reacted with abject dismay. Working another man's claim was not only bad manners but you could be hanged for it. Comstock, as generous with words as with his imagination, kindly allowed them to work his "claim" on a percentage basis. Thus, by a claim which has since proved a virtual fraud, the hitherto despised Washoe diggings became the Comstock Lode, a source of silver which founded, among others, the fortunes of George Hearst, John Mackay, and other multimillionaires—fortunes which financed the Civil War, caused Bismarck to order Germany off the silver standard, and reduced silver to the state of a base metal throughout the world. The Nevada mining boom built the transcontinental railways, laid the Atlantic cable, and established sourdoughs as prominent bank presidents, ambitious newspaper publishers, and tycoons, who married their children to European titles.

Virginia City, which grew up around the original strike, became a source of incalculable riches. How it got its name is a fact attested to by history and by hearsay. One epic Saturday night while the camp was still young, a lovable derelict named James Finney was wending his way to his shack after a particularly alcoholic evening. Finney was a man of seedy grandeur. He was from Virgina, he said, and spoke with a Southern accent to prove it. In appearance he was the forerunner of all the Southern colonels pictured with white mustache and goatee, seated on a veranda. Finney's aptitude for self-dramatization resulted in his being known far and wide as "Old Virginny." On this Saturday night he stumbled happily along, clutching a bottle of stimulant as insurance against the hangover of the next day. A fearful catastrophe overtook him. Those within earshot heard a crash of glass and a splash of liquid against rock. This was followed immediately by the voice of Old Virginny raised first in lamentation, then wrath, ending with the moaning declaration that good liquor should not be wasted and if a cruel fate had taken it from him, then he should have a christening for his money. His voice boomed out oratorically but thickly, "I christen this ------ camp, Virginia!" The word spread and within a few days Virginia City was the accepted name of the village growing up around the Comstock Lode.

It is a fact that of the original adventurers of this area, none had the talent to profit from the incredible bonanza they had unearthed. Henry Comstock, who did manage to declare himself in on every discovery in the area, sold out his share of the fabulous Ophir Mine, which made billions, for a paltry eleven thousand dollars. A few years later, immersed in alcohol and debts, he shot himself. Old Virginny Finney, who named the queen city of the mighty Comstock, sold out for a quart of whiskey and a stone-blind mustang. He, too, found a pauper's grave while a new generation of Comstock multimillionaires swaggered through the pleasure markets of the world. As for Pat McLaughlin and Peter Reilly, they sold their piece of the Comstock Lode for forty thousand dollars, only to see it producing over seventeen million dollars a year almost immediately. McLaughlin got a job as cook on a Montana sheep ranch. Reilly died in a madhouse and was buried in a pauper's grave.

Perhaps the most pathetic story of the period was that of Alvah Gould, co-discoverer of the Gould-Curry mine which brought in millions. Arrogant, stupid, and a drunkard, he sold his share for four hundred and fifty dollars in cash and spent it in one glorious carousal while bragging to all how he had trimmed some suckers.

In retrospect, everything that happened in Nevada up to 1873 was mere child's play. By that year, the mines of the

Comstock had been in and out of bonanzas half a dozen times. After each slump there would be a new strike, and things boomed again. Virginia City was always either on top of the world or wallowing in a deep depression. Hysteria was the norm, sudden riches and sudden suicides the conventional order of things.

Entering for the stakes at this time were four men who, far from being ignorant prospectors, were extremely capable mine operators who believed there was more in the Comstock Lode than met the eye. These were James Flood, James Fair, John Mackay, and William S. O'Brien. In the middle of the Comstock Profile lay two mines, Consolidated Virginia and California. Mackay was obsessed with the idea, whether by intuition or special knowledge nobody knew, that there was extremely rich ore in these properties then considered worthless. With the three other men mentioned, he had little trouble buying control of the property. They worked it themselves and within a few weeks found a silver vein fully seven feet wide. They managed to keep this enormously rich find quiet while they continued to buy up remaining stock wherever they could. They continued to search out the mine and what they found next changed the course of world history. Within three hundred feet of their initial strike, Fair and Mackay cut into a block of pure silver fifty-four feet wide and of undetermined height and depth!

The normal thing would have been to shriek their discovery to the world, but the four partners kept the treasure a secret and continued to buy up stock. They blocked the bonanza and knew they were the richest men in the world. Then casually and deliberately they let the news leak out. James Fair called Dan DeQuille, mining editor of the *Territorial Enterprise*. He was an experienced mining reporter, trusted by all, with years of Comstock experience behind him.

"Dan!" Jim Fair said to him indignantly. "The San Francisco papers have been calling us fly-by-nights and common stock riggers. My partners and I, we resent this treatment. We want you to come down into Consolidated Virginia, and you just let the world know what you see."

DeQuille could not believe what he saw. So amazed and frightened was he at the sight of solid silver that he cut his original estimate of the ore in half. Even then he announced that nearly 116 million dollars worth of silver was "visible."

This was it. The four men became truly kings of the Comstock. They themselves became peers in the tradition of Croesus, the Incas, and the maharajahs of India. They became, in fact, the richest men of all time in the known world. Now it was time to live out the days of their wealth.

John Mackay, focal point of the partnership, had one prime enjoyment in life: he liked to play poker. Wealth made him sad for only one reason. As he remarked to Dan DeQuille one night, "What good is living if a man can't enjoy winning at cards. No amount of money I could conceivably win at cards could excite me. You know, Dan, once I said that when I made two hundred thousand dollars I would retire—that the man who wanted more was a fool. You think I'm just a rich fool?"

In reality Mackay was unaffected by his riches except to use them well. The wealth he wrested from the California and Consolidated Virginia mines was used to develop transcontinental railroads, the transatlantic cable, telegraph systems, sugar refineries, copper mills, and real estate, as well as donated to churches, schools, and other charities.

While Mackay bore the burden of his wealth in his own quiet way, his wife Marie had other ambitions. She set out to conquer the formal society of Europe, armed with limitless financial resources and a naïve determination to display them. Mackay was glad to have her go since the parties and grand balls she insisted on hostessing were a source of boredom and discomfort to him. He footed her European bills on the condition that he would not have to participate in her diversions. He would, however, visit his wife's palaces in London and Paris.

Possessed of a lively, though quiet, sense of humor, Mackay visited his wife and played the part of an uncouth American millionaire. In actuality, he was extremely well read, urbane, and a forceful tycoon in the world in which he lived. To Marie's embarrassment, he refused to be himself when in Europe. He absolutely refused to speak French, forcing his dinner partners to speak their stumbling English. Instead of the rare clarets and noble champagnes served by his wife's wine stewards, he would insist in a loud voice on a shot of straight bourbon with the pheasant. During dinner he would recall in a loud voice his boyhood days in Dublin, pointing out that his family's pig had shared the parlor in the best shanty-Irish tradition. To Marie's annoyance and humiliation, he enjoyed his rare visits enormously—but in his own way.

Mackay died in 1902. His business manager quite unconsciously gave him an epitaph when he told reporters, "I don't suppose Mackay knew within twenty million what he was worth."

Queen of the Comstock

When I was yet in grade school, Dr. Livingston C. Lord, the first president of the Eastern Illinois Normal School, came to my village to deliver an address for the one-room, two-year high school, "non-district" as it was called. In those days the roads were so bad that the students could not get to Newton, the county seat. Dr. Lord was a very dignified, old-fashioned, Eastern gentleman. His speech to us was fashioned, I now realize, to make the people in my village satisfied with their lot. Or better perhaps to say, not to pretend to be something other than what they were. He related a story, much to the enjoyment of my townsfolk: There was an ordinary man who by chance became very wealthy. The first thing he did was to buy a large limousine. He filled it with his large family and drove it to the center of the little town, one about the size of Hunt City, my town. He drove slowly through the village that all might see him and his family in all their glory. However, the citizens did not come out to see as he had expected, but remained indoors. Whereupon he stopped the car and called out in a loud voice: "Come everybody, look at us and see who we ain't."

MORE precious to the Nevada miners than dancing girls was Eilley Orrum. She was the first woman to set up a boardinghouse near the Comstock Lode. She washed the miners' shirts, cut their hair, and spread a table which became celebrated all along the foothills of the Sierras for its biscuits, beans, and the other substantial fare dear to the pioneer digestive tract.

Among her boarders was Sandy Bowers, one of the shrewdest of the early Comstockers. He had staked out a small footage in the center of the lode and stubbornly refused to part with it. Right next to Sandy's ten-foot claim was another ten-foot claim owned by his landlady, laundress, and favorite cook, Eilley Orrum.

Whether it was Sandy's aim to consolidate the two claims or insure the services of the only good cook in the territory is open to speculation. Perhaps the decision was Eilley's, for though she was a plain woman she had what she called "a mind of my own." She was not averse to marriage for she had come to Nevada from Salt Lake City where she had discarded two Mormon husbands, one a bishop of the Church of Latter-day Saints. In any case, Sandy and Eilley were married.

In no time at all, their mutual claim was being crushed at the rate of a hundred thousand dollars a month. The miner and his wife lost little time in demonstrating that money talks—and in a wondrously commanding voice.

Their first move was to build a palace befitting their wealth in a pleasant valley called "Washoe Meadows." The illiterate prospector settled down to enjoy himself. Eilley bought herself everything she could think of and then, through sheer boredom, took up crystal gazing. Sandy bought his wife the most expensive crystal in the East, and she soon became known for her powers as "The Washoe Seeress."

People came to visit the palace from far-off places. One and all exclaimed that no foreign castle or palace really could compare to Eilley's magnificent mansion. Now Eilley knew what royalty was. She decided that if her home were indeed a palace, then she certainly was as good as any queen. The more Eilley thought about it, the more convinced she was that she had much in common with her two cousins under the skin in Europe, Queen Victoria and the Empress Eugenie. Queens, she knew, often called on each other late in the afternoons for a cup of tea and a few tidbits of gossip about other queens in their palaces.

Eilley finally grew conscience-stricken at her own discourtesy. Manners demanded that she call on the queens of the courts of Europe. Sandy agreed.

They celebrated their departure by a lavish dinner at the International Hotel in Virginia City. Eilley said grandly to her old friends, "This little dinner is our way of saying fare-thee-well to our old acquaintances in the diggings."

Sandy made a farewell speech, standing on a fragile, French gilt chair. "We want everyone to have a good time and we have money to throw at the birds, so go ahead. Eilley and I seen some interesting people in our time around Washoe. We met up with Horace Greeley and Governor Nye and old Chief Winnemucca. Now we aim to see some even more interesting folk like the Queen of England on her throne. We'll be back, so drink hearty, everyone." And he stepped down to cheers.

One week and many toasts later, Sandy and Eilley left for San Francisco and the ship which would take them to England.

In London, Queen Eilley made it known to American Ambassador Charles Francis Adams that she wished to have tea with Queen Victoria. Try as he would, the good diplomat could not arrange for the presentation. As he explained to Queen Eilley, she was a divorced woman and therefore ineligible for the prim and proper Court of St. James.

Secretly sick at heart, Eilley maintained a smiling face and brought happiness to the merchants of Bond Street by spending money with wild abandon. As an indication of her resourcefulness in such a program, her drafts against Wells Fargo during their stay in Paris alone came to more than a quarter of a million dollars.

Before returning to America, Sandy and Eilley paid a visit to her family in Scotland. They were received with many reservations, for Eilley's kin did not believe a word of their story about silver. It was the opinion of the entire town that

Eilley had taken to piracy on the high seas. A few thought it might be counterfeiting.

Thwarted in her aching desire for tea with Queen Victoria, Eilley Bowers nonetheless returned triumphantly to Nevada: she returned clutching a package of cuttings from the Royal Ivy which overgrows the Royal Walls of Windsor Castle. Long after this Comstock queen grew tired of her priceless treasures—French mirrors, Italian statuary, bronzes, oil paintings, crystal chandeliers, Turkish carpets—she still took a delighted pride in the Royal Ivy which now grew luxuriously over the massive walls of Washoe Palace. In spite of the fact that Victoria had been prevented from meeting her, she regarded these cuttings as a personal gift, a royal token of kinship from a reigning monarch to another Very Exalted Personage.

A few years after their return, Sandy Bowers died and was buried in the hillside back of his splendid mansion in Washoe Meadows. A few years later, the Bowers claim ran out and Eilley, who had spent money as fast as it was made, was soon inviting picnickers to the mansion at so much per head. She also found it profitable to return to her former avocation of crystal gazing and made a fair living predicting good fortune in other people's lives.

Eilley lived to be an old lady, crippled, bent, and infirm. When debts finally forced her to give up the mansion and be taken to the old ladies' home, she was found trying to pull down the Royal Ivy that was growing on her walls. She fought fiercely when they stopped her. "Queen Victoria gave them to me. Queen of the Comstock I was," she wept and mumbled through toothless gums. "Nobody else can have them. They're Royal Ivy!"

Ultimately, Eilley was laid to rest beside her husband. At last report, the ivy still flourishes on the Bowers mansion, now a museum.

Wintering with Paul Bunyan

*When I came to write of Paul Bunyan—and no book on
America's past would be complete without Paul Bunyan—I was faced with a problem. Paul Bunyan was,
you see, both more than and less than a man. In one
way he was the dream of a logger sleeping the sleep
of the physically drained. In another he was a boast,
a wild exaggeration on a gigantic scale. And so I have
written this story as if I had been a logger, trying to
think and feel like one.*

I T WAS after the fall of the year when we came up the river.
The leaves were down and the wind had a good nip to it.
When we camped overnight, in the morning there was a
rime of frost over our blankets, and the fire felt good before the
sun came up.

We hit the deer track that we'd been told to look for just
above the first white water, and followed it to the tall timber
hills where the camp was. There was Pete, Harry, and myself
on our way to join Guy McCullum's crew. McCullum was logging new country that year and needed aplenty of hands. Work
aplenty and money aplenty for three young farm hands trying
to save enough to buy their own farms. Come winter with the
crops in and nothing but odd chores to do, and Pete, Harry,
and me would pack our kennebeckers and take off for the logging camps. Only that year it was different and exciting. We
were going up into new country never before logged.

The forest, the virgin timber, was all around us. There wasn't
a hoot of a train whistle nor the sight of a farmer's chimney
smoke to show where the wilderness ended. It made me think
of how it was when the trees stretched like a green tossing sea
around the prairies and deserts; when the forest flowed like a

river between the hills, drowning the valleys in leaves and needles; when the rivers had to tunnel their way through to get to the sea, and the night was filled from coast to coast with the voices of the forest talking to the wind.

The first hoarse, panting breaths of winter knocked the bare branches together over our heads. Our ears were so filled with the clashing and thrashing that after a while we didn't notice it any more than we noticed the noise the river made. The deer track was easy to follow, but looking off between the trees we could see how choked the spaces between the trunks were with fallen logs and branches and big spurs of rock poking up above the forest floor. It was all new logging country, not yet blazed by the surveyor's axe, hard country to log, filled with tall Norway pine and maple, birch, and mountain ash, and good stands of oak and spruce. Plenty of young timber, not too old for cutting, many and many board feet to float down the river to the mills. It was hard country to log, but just to walk through and look at it, was enough to set a logger's heart to beating fast.

We hit the camp just at dark, in time to hear the bull cook's call for grub. We ate salt pork, sourdough bread, and strong tea until we had enough. Then we went over to the bunkhouse and picked out three bunks. We were eight to a bunk in this camp, double-decker. Picking out a bunk wasn't just a matter of slinging your kennebecker onto it. The top bunks were the best, up where a man could punch a hole for extra air if the shanty got too stuffy. The thing you had to watch out for was bedcats. Not that you could expect to find a bunk without at least a few. That was to be expected in any camp no matter how clean it was kept. But you didn't want to wake up in the middle of the night to find that you'd moved in with a whole tribe of the varmints!

When we'd got settled, we joined the rest of the crew sitting around the shanty smoking and yarning. Pete took his axe over to the grindstone that sat in the middle near the big iron stove-box and started to set the edge a little sharper. Harry and me found spots on the deacon seats, the row of benches that ran around the edge of the lower bunks. They were about the only things in the shanty besides the bunks that could answer to the name of furniture. For the rest there was a big tank of water that connected to the stove for heating, and a couple of oil lamps hanging from the roof. Socks and shirts and things were hung around the stove and the water tank to dry.

McCullum had a good gang with him that year, loggers who had worked with him up on the Miramichi in New Brunswick or around Mount Katahdin in Maine. We knew most of them, fellows like Jesse Beach, who was bull of the woods for Mc-Cullum; Stacey Monroe, who'd boss the drive down-river come spring; Larry Gorum, a good man with axe or saw, who had a way with tunes and words that kept us happy and amused all through the winter.

Everybody was getting reacquainted with the work partners they hadn't seen since the previous spring.

It was, "Hey there, Joe, y'old bobcat, how'd you ever find your way up here?" and, "Sam, you still plowin' that l'il ol' rock patch you call a farm?" There were a few greenhorns around, their mouths open as wide as their ears while the old-timers did their best to stand their hair on end with tall tales about crashing timber and the strange creatures that live in the woods. The talk hummed and buzzed, the grindstones rasped on the axe edges, and a thin blue cloud of pipe smoke drifted over our heads. Every so often the stove hissed as some chawer let fly at the lid.

Then a logger came in from outside carrying an armful of logs for the stove and announced that it was snowing. We crowded to the door to look out. Sure enough, there was a thin film of white powder over everything, and in the light that streamed out through the open door the snow swirled and danced. The slight wind was icy cold, and the air smelled clean and fresh after the closeness of the shanty.

Snow meant logging time was at hand, and the talk ran to regular logging talk—how many lots had been falled last winter, the size of skid loads, the merits of different-make axes and saws, and so on. About nine o'clock McCullum came around to assign wood lots to the different gangs, for falling was to start next morning. By that time there'd be enough snow for the skids to slide on. The teamsters stepped out for a last look to the oxen and horses, and then it was time to put out the lights and crawl in between the blankets and the marsh grass mattress.

Outside there was the snowy sigh of the wind, inside the heavy breathing of the men. I lay awake for a while thinking about the woodlands we'd seen on the way to the camp. When I closed my eyes, I could see the tall columns of bark going up, up, straight up, till you had to crane your neck way back to see where the branches started. In my head I could see the figures of men among the trees, barrel-chested, broad-shouldered, muscle-backed men like those who slept around me. I could see them through the forest, and against the trunks of the trees, they looked too small and puny to ever bring those giants crashing to the ground.

By and by, all the men started to melt in together making a monster figure that kept growing and growing as the men in my half-dream kept blending into him. Just before I fell off to sleep I saw him towering above the treetops, Mackinawed and bearded, combing his hair with a pine tree. His axe had a hickory tree for a handle, and the cutting edge was three miles long. Paul Bunyan, it was. And my giant looked out over the forest and he threw back his head and he laughed till the trees bent their tops in the gale of his laughing. Then he swung his axe and the timber fell in wood lots, in great, wide swaths. And he opened his mouth and he shouted . . .

"Roll out! Roll out, you loggers! Time to let some daylight into that swamp! Roll out!"

But when I rubbed my eyes open, it was the bull cook's voice I heard as he walked through the camp beating on the chuck hammer, rousing us out of our bunks.

The drivers were up already tending the stock. We had a quick wash and went on out to the cookshack. There was over a foot of snow down by that time, and more on the way. We knocked the snow off our boots and sat down to buckwheat cakes, hash, warmed-over potatoes, steak, fried salt pork, cold beans, tea, black coffee with brown sugar, eggs, mush, and prune pie. Nobody talked while we ate, that's the rule in all logging camps. The flunkeys kept filling the serving bowls or passing along fresh pitchers of coffee and stacks of cakes.

After grub, we went back to the shanty and sat around waiting for the foreman to call us out. Pipes were lit and we sat around easy, giving our breakfast a chance to settle.

Harry griped a little. He said the cookshack should have at least two stoves so there'd be more stove lids to make the buckwheat cakes on. Said it took too long for a fellow to get seconds and thirds if he had to wait till everybody had firsts.

Pete laughed and ribbed him some.

"What you want is a cookshack with a griddle about a mile long and twice again as wide."

"That's not a bad idea. If ever I run a logging camp that's how the cookshack'll be laid out."

Harry looked and sounded so serious that one of the greenhorns stared hard at him.

"How d'ja 'spect to get a griddle that size greased? 'Pears like by the time one side is ready t'other end'll need greasin' again."

Harry waved a disparaging hand.

"That's no problem. I'd take and cut me some good, thick ham steaks. Then I'd strop those steaks to Cookee's feet and let 'im skate all over that griddle till she was greased just right."

"Daylight in the swamp!" bawled the bull from outside. "Let's get that timber cut!"

We left the greenhorn scratching his head, joined our gang, and headed for the tall pines. It had stopped snowing for a spell and the temperature had gone away down. The axes began to swing and bite, and the saws commenced to rip their way through the wood. It wasn't any time at all before the woods rang to "Widow maker!" and "Timber-r-r!" followed by the crash and thump of the first timbers to hit ground.

There is quite an art to falling trees the way we did. First a notch is cut with the inside edge straight. Then the chopper or sawyer sets to work with axe or saw from the opposite side and cuts in towards the notch. The tree always falls towards the notch. We'd aim it so the trunk wouldn't hit into another tree or split on a rock. Every so often a saw would get pinched in the trunk and a sawyer would have to tap in an iron wedge to take up the pressure.

Once the tree was down we'd trim off the branches, and a barker would strip the rear end to make it drag easier. We'd get one end up on one of those little sleds we called a go-devil, and the team would pull it down a skidway to a spot where cant-hook men would load them onto the big skids.

Must've been about ten or fifteen above, but in no time at all we were all of us sweating under our Mackinaws and heavy wool pants. Later on it was to go down below zero, so cold that our breaths would freeze and we'd have to melt off the icicles from our beards before we could eat.

While we were falling trees, the swampers were building skid roads by clearing off underbrush and packing down the snow, so's to make a roadbed that led in the straightest possible line to the river bank. Where they hit swampy spots they would lay beds of logs corduroy fashion and pack snow on top. Then they'd pour water over the whole thing and, when the ice had formed, cut grooves all the way along for the skid runners. In the meantime, we'd be putting chains on, and, when that huge pile of lumber, tons of it, was balanced on the skid, the driver would start her down the road to the river.

Driving those loads along a slippery road like that was some stunt. I'd a lot rather cut timber than drive a skid. Too tricky and dangerous, too liable to tip. Happened aplenty of times the whole load of logs slipped sideways and fell and the teamster jumped and dodged for very life. I'll take my chances with widow makers.

Came noontime and we got the call "Take the bait!" The foreman had a clear spot marked off with split logs for benches and a big kettle of water going over a good fire. Cookee came along with the grub wrapped in blankets on a bobsled. Mostly the lunch was slumgullion—good old meat stew!—with bread and hot tea.

It sure was good that first day to sit or stand around a fire in the middle of the woods, stuffing ourselves on slumgullion, washing it down with blazing hot tea. Later on, lunchtime got to be just something necessary; not that we objected to food, but it meant eating with our gloves on and having to eat real fast before the food froze to the tin plates.

We worked on all that afternoon. Nobody rushed us. The work just got done: the trees came down, were stripped, and hauled away. When dark began to gather, we slung our tools over our shoulders and hiked back to camp, tired and hungry. It sure felt real good to sit down in that warm cook shanty, stretch our legs under the table and reach out for the grub. There was pea soup, potatoes, beans, greens, smoked ham, bread and butter, and big prune and apple pies, followed up by tea strong enough to eat the top of our pine table, and cookies, the big kind with sugar sprinkled all over them.

The menus never varied much, but nobody complained. Not that we loggers don't complain about food. What goes on in the cookshack is the most important thing in the world to us. God help the cook who doesn't suit our tastes. He'd pack his turkey sack and hit the road pretty soon, and there's not much logging done until he does! This camp was good, and we didn't do much griping about grub that winter. Once, on a Sunday, Pete and I went out hunting. We got a big buck, and the whole camp had a change that tasted almighty good.

Come spring we got a little tired of pea soup. Matter of fact, we couldn't figure out where all that soup was coming from, till Pete explained it. His explanation satisfied all but the greenhorns. You see, there was a big hot spring a mile or so from camp. Pete claimed that when they were bringing up grub supplies one of the flunkeys spilled a whole load of dried split peas into this spring. Not wanting to waste all those peas, Cookee got the bright idea of dumping in appropriate amounts of soup greens and the other ingredients—thus assuring the camp of a winter's supply of hot pea soup. The only catch was having to send a couple of miles for the soup every day.

The greenhorns didn't believe a word of Pete's story. Leastwise, they didn't look like they did, though none of them dared to say anything. Just the same Jesse Beach caught one of them sneaking back to camp early one day. Said he wanted to see where the cook got the soup from, his big kettle or the hot spring.

The days and weeks went by, and the logs by the riverside piled high and aplenty. The work got pretty dull, like any backbreaking job does when you're at it for so long without a break. All day we worked without saying more to each other than we had to. We talked less and less at night, and most of us were asleep before curfew. It was like everybody had put his head down and braced himself to work away hard and get the job done soon as possible.

I remember Pete stopping one day after we'd finished putting our company brand on a tree and looking around. Behind us was a slope cut clean. Down ahead we could see a skid load headed for the river.

"Ain't it a shame!" says Pete.

"Ain't what a shame?" I asked.

"If there was only a way to get this timber to the river without there being so much work to it."

Harry squinted a little like he does when he's thinking.

"How would it be," he said slowly, "if we was to put a chain around, oh, say about forty lots, haul them to river, and cut all the trees right at the water 'stead of back up here!"

Pete nodded soberly like the idea had real merit to it, like it was real practical. "Reckon you'd need a good-size ox for that," he opined.

"Not so big," said Harry. "A medium-size big feller, measuring, say, six or seven axe handles."

I stuck my neck way out. "You mean long? That ain't so much of an ox."

"Not long. Between the eyes! Come on, let's strip this here tree!"

All the rest of that afternoon I had a kind of mental picture of us putting a chain around a big section of woodland and having this tremendous ox pull it down to the river for stripping, like taking a sheep to be sheared. Remembering the big logger I'd dreamed of the first night in camp, I put him next to the ox in my mind and I agreed—that they'd make a fine pair.

You shoulda seen O'Conner, our bunkmate, who was still green. He'd never heard such talk. Of course, we were joking about our big logger, Paul Bunyan, like the one I'd dreamed up one night, and his giant ox, Babe. Bunyan—a kind of made-up character, made up so big he can do anything easy that we do hard and sweat over.

Saturday nights we'd break the monotony the best way we could, being up in the woods away from towns and women. We'd forget curfew, and Larry Gorum would take out his accordion, and maybe somebody'd have a mouth organ. Some of the men would wear rags or towels around their middles, and we'd get up a stag dance. Between dances we'd sit around and join in with Larry as he sang songs about the camps, or rivermen, or lonely loves on snowy hilltops. Larry had a song he'd made up about being at Burns's log camp:

> *I 'rived in the camp, and all I could see*
> *Was a lousy old cook and a lousy Cookee;*
> *The floors were all dirty, all covered with mud;*
> *The bed quilts were lousy, and so was the grub.*
>
> *The cook called for supper; they all tore from work.*
> *Some had two knives and other two forks.*
> *While fighting for molasses, they upset the lamp,*
> *And thus I was greeted at Burns's log camp.*

One of our favorite songs, and I can't write down most of the verses because the page would burn up, was "The Red Light Saloon." It started something like this:

A trip down to Bangor, the Fourth of July:
To make my connection with a train I did try.
The train it being late, as you all will know soon,
I was forced to take a trip to the Red Light Saloon.

I boldly walked in and stepped up to the bar,
When a saucy young damsel says, "Have a cigar!"
A cigar I did take, in a chair I sit down,
When a saucy young damsel came tripping around.

She boldly came over, sit down on my knee,
Saying, "Jack, you're a woodsman, that I plainly see."
Saying, "Jack, you're a woodsman, and that we all know.
Your muscle is hard from your head to your toe! . . .

Sundays we'd rest, sharpen tools, mend clothes and equipment, or boil our socks. Some joker would set himself up as a barber and the old shears would go clip, clip around the edge of a big soup bowl. Or we'd go to the wanigan, a sort of camp office and store where we could buy tobacco, and knives, and sometimes even clothes. Otherwise it was just plain loafing and resting weary backs and muscles, preparing for another week in the woods.

Once in a while, one of the men brought in some corn and we'd have a brawl. My dad was from Pennsylvania and he used to say there were three kinds of drinkers—squirrel, fighting, and sleeping. One kind, the squirrel, drank and wanted to climb trees. The other drinkers just followed what the words meant. We had all kinds at camp that winter. I'm a sleeper myself.

Finally, it was spring thaw. The logging was done. Most of the men slung their kennebeckers over their shoulders and started on home. That year though, Harry, Pete, and me stayed on for the river drive. McCullum was paying bonus money to get those logs down to the sawmills. He had thousands of board feet to handle, was short-handed and needed help getting it down to the mills.

On the day after the river was free of ice, we took our places along the banks below the high piles of logs. A couple of jerks with a peavey on the key logs. Sssssss——crash! and the pile would go sliding into the stream with big sheets of water spraying up all around.

Down the river went the logs spinning like mad, with us riding along, our cleated boots digging into the slippery bark, our feet twirling till they were a blur to watch as we kept our footing and the logs moving at the same time. It was tricky, dangerous work. We rode the logs through rapids, between cakes of floating ice, around narrow bends and in between submerged rocks, over half-sunk logs and sandspits. Sometimes we fell in the water. There we had to scramble to the bank or back upon a log aplenty fast before we got hit or crushed by the logs around us.

The drive went on fine . . . until the third day. Coming around a turn with white water ahead, the lead logs caught on a row of rocks and everything jammed up behind. The river kept pushing the logs on down, and they piled up one on top the other until there was a towering height of logs while behind the jam three miles more of logs pushed down on the whole creaking mass. Worst jam I ever saw.

Stacey Monroe, who was in charge of the drive, rode out on a log right under the face of the jam, cool as you please, looking the situation over. When he got back to shore, he asked us for volunteers to help him set a charge of dynamite. He didn't want to take any chances pulling and probing for key logs, not with all that back tonnage.

Nobody moved for a bit, not even when McCullum offered a whopping big bonus. Then, before we could stop him, Harry said, "What the hell! We'll never get to home at this rate!" and he stepped out to Monroe's side.

I stood on that river's edge and watched them walk out over

the jam. Just before they got to where the trouble was the center kind of rumbled and sunk in on itself. But the jam held.

Monroe and Harry waited and then went on. When they got to midstream they worked their way down the face of the jam and set the charge. Monroe was an old hand at this kind of thing, so he cut the fuse and lit it. Then they started to run back, hopping from log to log fast as they could.

We watched the two figures move over that sea of logs holding our breath and not moving. Behind them there was that wisp of smoke where the fuse sputtered and burned away.

Suddenly a yell! Harry was down in a hole! His foot was caught between two logs. Stacey, a little ahead, heard the yell and turned back. Pete and me didn't wait for an invitation—we started out onto the jam. A couple of the men followed.

We could see Stacey trying to lever a log with his peavey so Harry could get loose. Harry helped all he could but it was plain it would take more than them two to lift a couple of tons of dead weight. We cursed and prayed, clambering over and around logs, hopping the holes fast as we could. Then Monroe left Harry and ran back towards the middle of the jam. I thought he had chickened out and losing his head had run in the wrong direction. Then I saw what he was up to. He was trying to reach that charge before it went off!

Pete was halfway from shore—I was much behind—when the charge exploded. Pete kept going but I stopped and looked for Monroe. I had a glimpse of him halfway down the face of the jam being lifted up by the blast just as the weight started to settle back in. He threw up his hands as a big pine unbalanced and slid off the top just above him. Then the whole face gave and it crumbled with a roar and he was lost in a cracking and crashing of logs and water.

The logs began to move. Pete reached Harry just as the logs around him got in motion. He grabbed Harry under the arms and hoisted. By that time I was too busy running on a spinning log to pay them much heed. When I looked again they were both riding the tree just ahead of me.

Nothing we could do about Monroe. That afternoon we reached the first booms above the sawmills where the river widened. Monroe's body had got caught here. We buried him at sundown on a shady knoll looking over the river. Not having a chaplain nor a church close enough, it was, "Ashes to ashes and dust to dust. May he rest in peace. Cover him up, boys!"

That night, to cheer us up, Larry sang us a song about a drive that went down a river that kept doubling back on itself. The loggers kept driving the logs past the same camp time after time until they finally caught wise that they were driving along a round river. It was a good song and it made us smile. Only Harry sat there by the fire rubbing his leg where it was pinched and not saying much. I saw him get up and limp off into the dark before the song was through.

This was the place we rafted in. The water was quiet here. We put the logs side by side, eighty feet long some of them were, and attached 'em to a lash pole with U-shaped spikes that were held to the logs with pins. A part of this raft we used as a platform and covered it with stones and earth. Then we put up a tent and had a snug little place to sleep, cook, and eat.

We were lucky to have Jim Beck, one of the great raft pilots, with us. He could, and he sure did, make a raft take every rock, every bend, every current easy and smooth.

A week later all the timber was at the sawmill, thousands and thousands of trees stretching from bank to bank and upstream and out of sight. McCullum paid us off, and Pete, Harry, and me started for the depot. We were aiming to leave soon as the train came through.

We walked along the only street of that sawmill town lined with saloons and general stores. The men weren't wasting any time blowing in their pay. The town screamed with loggers letting off steam after a winter in the wilderness. They filled the air with wild yells and snatches of song, and there were more'n a couple of shrill female voices mixed in the fun, too.

We got to the end of the street at the top of a little rise and stopped to look back at the river. We could see the mill below us and the logs. We followed with our eye the banks of the stream where the water shone like silver between the trees. To the north were the timber-covered hills. Harry cleared his throat.

"Reckon we'll come back next year? Hear McCullum's goin' to run the same camp."

"Aplenty of timber left up there," Pete said. "If Guy don't get it someone else will."

We turned away and went on. The spring was ahead of us for plowing and planting, and the summer heat, and then the fall harvest before we'd pack our turkey sacks again and head north. In all those months we'd spend in the rich valleys of home, the timberlands would be up there quiet and still waiting for the sound of the axe to return. And in that time, Pete, Harry, and me would spend many an evening telling the home folks about the logging camps.

We'd tell how virgin timber country looks, how lonely and still it is with only miles of woods all around, and every mile lacking homesteads. We'd tell about the falling and the hauling, how big the pine and hemlock is, and how the skids slide down to the river. We'd tell about the other men in the camp, about the credulous greenhorns and the great choppers and swampers. And if I chose to tell a few tall ones, about the inexhaustible supply of pea soup, about the size of our hotcake griddle and how we went driving round and round a river without end . . . and if I should tell about the big logger standing with his head above the trees and his blue ox that dragged acres of woodland to the river for falling . . . why, I don't think Pete and Harry would do any more than wink at each other!

And if the folks thought those were whoppers . . . why just let 'em.

"He Died Hard"

Something has gone from the American scene now that we no longer have a cavalry division in our army. The horse was more than a romantic element in the American frontier. The scout, who was in the forefront of the Conestoga train and who served the American Army so well in fighting the militant Indian tribes of the West, depended on his horse as on himself. Poor Bill Cody learned this lesson in a very embarrassing way.

T HE plainsmen were the cream of American horsemen. The relationship that existed between riders and mounts was a deep one, based on mutual trust and dependency. The horses were the mustangs of the Western plains, the pintos, the claybanks, and the buckskins. These were the horses that descended from those ridden years ago by Spanish conquerors. These were the horses that bred and grew into herds of twenty to thirty thousand head. These were the hardy mounts the Plains Indians roped and tamed and taught to hunt buffalo and ride the warpath.

Buffalo Bill Cody, in his early days as buffalo hunter and Indian army scout and pony express rider, rode a variety of these horses. Indeed, he was famous for his selection of horses and liked nothing better than to match his mounts against any comer.

One of his famous horses was Powder Face, a nervous animal, hard to manage under any circumstances. One day at Fort Sedgwick, Cody matched Powder Face against a fast pony owned by a man named Luke North. North mounted a Pawnee lad as his jockey. Not to be outdone, Cody selected a

279

small boy who lived on the post and was about equal in weight.

The starting signal so aroused Powder Face that he threw his rider at the outset. Then he raced down the course, crossing the finish line far in the lead. Cody insisted on collecting—and over North's objections, he did.

Another of his famous horses was Tall Bull, whom he captured in a battle with the Kiowa Indians. Cody named Tall Bull after the Indian chief that he had shot from the horse's back.

With his reputation for fast horses and fast traveling, it is not surprising to hear of a feat of horsemanship of remarkable endurance and courage performed by Cody. It was during the campaign with the Comanche tribes. In less than sixty hours, he rode 350 miles, carrying dispatches from Fort Larned to Fort Hays, then from Fort Hays to Fort Dodge, Kansas, from Fort Dodge to Fort Larned and finally from Larned back to Hays. This extraordinary performance was rewarded by General Sheridan, who was in command at Fort Hays. Sheridan cited Cody in dispatches, appointed him chief scout of his command, and later included a full report of the incident in his memoirs.

It was because of his reputation with horses that Cody was particularly humiliated by an experience that happened in Indian territory, and well might have cost him his scalp.

An important message had to go from Fort Dodge to Fort Larned. Cody was the most likely man to go through. He received his orders and sent for his horse. Imagine his distress on learning that his horse was lame and no other was available. In desperation, he saddled up one of the army mules.

He rode out of the post at dark and covered some thirty miles before dismounting to rest at a creek. As he bent down to fill his hat with water, he was pulled off balance. The mule suddenly jerked away, pulling the reins from Cody's grasp, and made off down the bank of the stream! He headed straight for an old wagon road. Cody had been avoiding this road deliberately for fear that the wily Kiowa Indians had it under observation. Now he had no other choice than to pursue his mount on this same open road.

Once on the road, the mule went east, in the direction of Fort Larned. Cody cussed and chased and chased and cussed, but to no avail. When he tried to catch up by running, the mule trotted. When Cody walked, the mule walked too.

The absurd chase continued for thirty-five miles. The enraged, tired, and exasperated Cody ached to shoot the stubborn animal. He would have, too, but he had no wish to call the attention of the Kiowa braves to his dismounted condition.

At dawn as the morning gun was fired, the sentries of Fort Larned called the fort's attention to a strange sight. Out of the still-dark west, a strange twosome came through the sagebrush and mesquite. There was a mule, saddled and bridled. Behind him limped a man.

Dust-covered, footsore, and cursing a blue streak, was Cody, looking like a rabbit chasing a carrot at the end of a stick.

A few hundred yards from the fort, Cody took his revenge. Raising his gun to his shoulder, he blasted that army mule to kingdom come.

Cody drank deeply, delivered his message. When he stepped out among the men, nobody smiled. He looked at them in disgust. A stream of unprintable phrases ended in the mule's epitaph. Cody said, "He was the toughest and meanest mule anybody ever saw. And he died hard!"

Minstrel Making

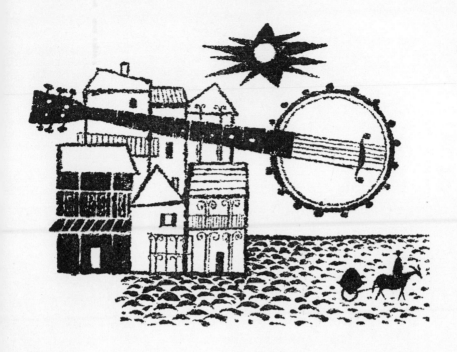

When I was a boy in grade school a hometown play was put on called Misery Moon, the Hoodooed Coon. *I was chosen to play the lead, and between the acts I sang some minstrel songs. This was the first time I ever wore burnt cork. After that memorable debut, I performed in minstrel shows many times—at county fairs and in Midwestern towns like Terre Haute, Indiana—and I have always had a great love for them. Strange as it may seem, I have never seen one. But in my mind's eye I have attended many since their beginning in this country. The minstrel show is completely American. This story will shed a little light on how it began.*

IT WAS a sultry, humid night in New Orleans in the year 1861. The Civil War, like every war, had generated a live-today-for-tomorrow-we-die hysteria, and people were spending their money, throwing parties, drinking—and going to the theater. On this night the Varieties Theater was crowded to capacity, and the bill promised to be a good one:

MRS. JOHN WOOD,

The Celebrated Actress will appear in a Special

Performance of

POCAHANTAS

Written by that Famous Author

JOHN BROUGHAM

* * *

The Gala Finale Will be a

Zouave March

Complete With

MILITARY BAND AND FURLED FLAGS

* * *

The night was warm, the theater close, and the audience grew impatient before the end of *Pocahantas*, excellent as Mrs. Wood's portrayal was. They were apathetic even when the Zouaves first marched on stage, magnificent in their regimental uniforms. Then the band struck up the tune which was known to some of the theatergoers as a minstrel turn. It was called "Dixie's Land." As the choruses followed one after the other in march tempo, the audience, wide-awake now, began to sing:

Southrons, hear your country call you!
Up, lest worse than death befall you!
   To arms! To arms! To arms, in Dixie.
Lo! all the beacon fires are lighted,
Let all hearts be now united!
   To arms! To arms! To arms, in Dixie.

CHORUS:

Advance the flag of Dixie! Hurrah! Hurrah!
For Dixie's land we take our stand, and live and die for Dixie!
To arms! To arms! And conquer peace for Dixie!
To arms! To arms! And conquer peace for Dixie!

Hear the Northern thunders mutter!
Northern flags in South winds flutter!
   To arms! To arms! To arms, in Dixie.
Send them back your fierce defiance!
Stamp on the accursed alliance!
   To arms! To arms! To arms, in Dixie.

Fear no danger! Shun no labor!
Lift up rifle, pike and sabre!
   To arms! To arms! To arms, in Dixie.
Shoulder pressing close to shoulder,
Let the odds make each heart bolder!
   To arms! To arms! To arms, in Dixie.

How the South's great heart rejoices,
At your cannons' ringing voices!
    To arms! To arms! To arms, in Dixie.
For faith betrayed, and pledges broken,
Wrongs inflicted, insults spoken,
    To arms! To arms! To arms, in Dixie.

Strong as lions, swift as eagles,
Back to their kennels hunt these beagles!
    To arms! To arms! To arms, in Dixie.
Cut the unequal bonds asunder!
Let them hence each other plunder!
    To arms! To arms! To arms, in Dixie.

Swear upon your country's altar
Never to submit or falter!
    To arms! To arms! To arms, in Dixie.
Till the spoilers are defeated,
Till the Lord's work is completed.
    To arms! To arms! To arms, in Dixie.

Halt not till our Federation
Secures from earth's powers its station!
    To arms! To arms! To arms, in Dixie.
Then at peace, and crowned with glory,
Hear your children tell the story!
    To arms! To arms! To arms, in Dixie.

If the loved ones weep in sadness,
Victory soon will bring them gladness.
    To arms! To arms! To arms, in Dixie.
Exultant pride soon banish sorrow;
Smiles chase tears away tomorrow,
    To arms! To arms! To arms, in Dixie.

The audience left the theater in tremendous excitement. "Dixie's Land" became the patriotic hymn of the Confederacy almost overnight. The new words to the old minstrel tune were published in every Confederate newspaper. As a newspaper reporter of the period wrote, "Within weeks the saloons, parlors, streets and barracks are ringing with the 'Dixie' air and 'Dixie' has become to the South what the 'Marseillaise' is to France."

The writer of the original minstrel song, "Dixie's Land," was Daniel Decatur Emmett. That his song should have become the rallying song of the South was a great embarrassment to him. More than that, it proved a downright menace to his safety. For you see, Dan Emmett was a Northerner and a loyal Union man. From his youth he had been a devoted worker in the underground railway which helped thousands of Negroes to escape slavery. He was also, in 1861, respected as a top song writer and minstrelman. Imagine how he felt now that his most popular composition had become the rallying call of the Rebels, and New York audiences had turned against him. He could not walk down a New York street without hearing "The traitor . . . hang him!" or "That's Dan Emmett. He wrote 'Dixie' for the Rebels. He should be locked up!" or "Go back to the South, you Rebel. Go back where you came from!"

Poor Dan Emmett. A quiet, unassuming man, he could not shout back that he had come from Mount Vernon, Ohio, any more than he could shout back that he had written 'Dixie' two years before as a minstrel song, not a war song.

On the afternoon that New York learned that he was the composer of the Rebel song, Dan was lucky to get back to his boardinghouse in one piece. It was a tortuous thought to him as he went into his room that his friends back in Mount Vernon, Ohio, were probably also under the impression that he had written "Dixie" against the Union.

Sitting at the window of his boardinghouse room on lower Broadway, he looked back on his boyhood in Ohio. In 1830, when he had just turned fifteen, he had made his first public appearance. Music had been his chief occupation and pre-occupation since he had been a child. He was determined by the time he was fifteen to be a song-and-dance man. If he could not do this, he had decided to be a musician in a traveling band, for he could play the violin. A more secret ambition had to do with writing songs. He had written several but he kept them hidden under the mattress of his bed. On a summer day in 1830, he was appearing in public at the County Fair.

At the County Fair the crowd gathered around the bandstand as the entertainers came on one by one. Finally, a young man in burnt-cork blackface strutted out. None of his neighbors recognized him, not even his own parents, though they said later that he looked "kinda familiar like." The blackface artist played a quick chorus on his fiddle and then sang the words to a song nobody had heard before. They could not have heard it for Emmett had written it especially for his momentous debut. The name of the song was "Old Dan Tucker":

> *I come to town de udder night,*
> *I hear de noise, den saw de sight,*
> *De watchmen dey (was) runnin' roun',*
> *Cryin' "Ole Dan Tucker's come to town."*
> > *Git outen de way, git outen de way,*
> > *Git outen de way, Ole Dan Tucker,*
> > *You's too late to come to your supper.*

This seemed to be the end of the song and the crowd began to stomp and cheer. It was not, however, and the young man sang on and on until he had finished all the verses he had written . . . and a few extemporaneous ones besides:

> *Sheep an' hog a walkin' in de pasture,*
> *Sheep says, "hog can't you go faster?"*
> *Hush! hush! honey, hear de wolf growlin',*
> *Ah, ah, de Lawd, bull dog growlin'.*
> > *Git outen de way, git outen de way,*
> > *Git outen de way, Ole Dan Tucker,*
> > *You's too late to come to your supper.*

> *Here's my razor in good order,*
> *Magnum Bonum—jis hab bought 'er;*
> *Sheep shell oats, an' Tucker shell de corn,*
> *I'll shabe ye soon as de water gits warm.*
> > *Git outen de way, git outen de way,*
> > *Git outen de way, Ole Dan Tucker,*
> > *You's too late to come to your supper.*

Tucker went roun' hickry steeple,
Dar he meet some colored people,
Some was black, some was blacker.
Some was de color ob brown tobackur.
    Git outen de way, git outen de way,
    Git outen de way, Ole Dan Tucker,
    You's too late to come to your supper.

Jay bird in de martin's nest,
To sabe he soul he got no rest.
Ole Tucker in de foxe's den,
Out come de young ones nine or ten,
    Git outen de way, git outen de way,
    Git outen de way, Ole Dan Tucker,
    You's too late to come to your supper.

Tucker on de wood pile can't count lebben;
Put 'im in a fedder bed goin' to hebben;
His nose so flat, his face so full,
De top ob his head like a bag ob wool.
    Git outen de way, git outen de way,
    Git outen de way, Ole Dan Tucker,
    You's too late to come to your supper.

High-hold on de holler tree,
He poke his bill in for to see,
De lizard cotch 'im by de snout,
He call for Tucker to pull 'im out
    Git outen de way, git outen de way,
    Git outen de way, Ole Dan Tucker,
    You's too late to come to your supper.

I went to de meetin' de udder day
To hear ole Tucker preach and pray;
Dey all got drunk, but me alone,
I make ole Tucker walk jaw bone.
    Git outen de way, git outen de way,
    Git outen de way, Ole Dan Tucker,
    You's too late to come to your supper.

The applause was deafening. After the sixth encore, his dog Tucker—whose name he had combined with his own in the song—romped on the stage and demanded attention. It was then his father knew who the successful performer was.

The boy lifted his dog, who began to lick the burnt-cork face. Still holding the dog, Dan walked off the bandstand, determined now about his future life. It was going to be the theater.

There was a great deal of crying and scolding at home. Mrs. Emmett declared that the Emmetts were descendants of Virginia settlers who had fought in the American Revolution. Her own side, she said, had pioneered across the Blue Ridge Mountains and then across the Alleghenies to the Ohio. On both sides of Dan's family the men were farmers and gentlemen, not roustabouts. Mr. Emmett had to agree with his wife that traveling with shows was no life for a man with dignity. But Dan's mind was made up and finally he ran off with a circus band. In two years he associated with such famous road shows as those of Spaulding and Rogers, Seth Howe, and Dan Rice. However, in 1832 there was a lull in show business and at the age of seventeen he joined the army as a fifer.

Joining the army led him to the turning point of his life. The army stationed him near Philadelphia. He was not there more than two days when he heard that the famous "Daddy" Rice was doing his Jim Crow act at the leading variety theater in the City of Brotherly Love. Young Emmett used every power of persuasion to get the leave that was not due him for another few weeks. A few days later he was sitting in the first row watching his hero. He had never enjoyed anything so much nor envied anyone so completely. The audience cheered and clapped, and Emmett himself was hysterical with enthusiasm. After the show he ventured backstage to see the performer who was at once his idol and his ideal.

"Come in, son," Daddy Rice welcomed the young soldier who stood quivering in the dressing-room doorway. "Come in! come in! Make yourself comfortable. Tell me about yourself while I take this black muck off. What you doing in the army, boy?"

"I'm a fifer, sir. But when I get my discharge, I'm going back to trouping."

"Back to trouping! Why, my boy, you don't look old enough to have started," the star replied condescendingly, forgetting for the moment that he was still in his twenties himself and a headliner for only the last few of his many years as a trouper.

Emmett regained some of his spirit now that the initial newness of the situation had worn off. He answered eagerly, "I write songs and sing and dance. I can play the violin, and I wear blackface, too."

"That's a lot of talent for a youngster. Remember, though, there's lots of young men with talent. You gotta find a formula. There's a magic combination makes you a headliner instead of just a second-stringer. It's just that extra special something— call it luck, inspiration, or just the right minute. I tell you, when that happens, you can feel the audience sitting right in the palm of your hand. I have it, brother, but I didn't have it and I know."

Emmett's admiring gaze took in the handsome six-foot figure, noted the assured manner and the poise with which he pronounced his philosophy of performing. He wondered if he could ever become such a personality. "Mr. Rice, could you tell me how you became a headliner and how you came to write the Jim Crow song?"

Now it happened that Thomas Dartmouth "Daddy" Rice enjoyed nothing better than retelling the happy experience which had led to his present prominence. As he reached for his trousers, he began the tale:

"I was born in New York, my boy, and my parents apprenticed me to a wood carver in my early youth. My artistic temperament was not suited to such a limited endeavor, and I elected to run away and become an actor.

"For ten years I roamed this fair land, singing, dancing, earning my way with song. I must say at this period the ladies were much more appreciative of me after the show than the audience was during it. I should say that at that time I was one of those pleasant performers nobody remembers long enough to actively like or dislike. Then came the miracle!

"It was a gift of fate! A magic set of circumstances occurred." Carried away by his own eloquence, Rice walked up and down the room, waving his hands in demonstration. "I was going walking along a Cincinnati street early one morning when I passed a Negro stage driver lolling lazily on his box high above the street. His skin glistened black, his teeth were shiny white. Only his clothes were shabby and disreputable. As I stood near the stage, I could hear him chanting a little rhyme:

> *Turn about an' wheel about and do jiss so,*
> *An' ebery time I turn about I jump Jim Crow.*

"I tell you, boy, I couldn't get that little couplet out of my mind. I was singing it in my sleep and humming it at mealtime. Then came that magic.

"It happened this way. We closed in Cincinnati and our next date was Pittsburgh. In Pittsburgh the troupe always stays at the Griffiths Hotel on Wood Street. It was there I had the fortunate circumstance of becoming acquainted with a Negro named Cuff. . . ."

Emmett broke in, "You mean Cuff was a real person?"

"That he was," Rice assured him. He warmed to his recital. "Now this Cuff got his living by allowing little boys to pitch pennies into his mouth at three paces. He kept all the pennies regardless of whether they hit the target or not. Beside that he carried trunks off the Monongahela steamboat for the passengers who came in each day.

"It was that afternoon that somehow from seeing Cuff and remembering that 'jump Jim Crow' that I got The Idea! I took Cuff down to the theater with me before curtain time and made him take off all his clothes. Boy, I put on blackface for the first time then. Then I put on Cuff's old coat and his shoes. Boy, you should have seen those shoes! They were just patches and places for patches. Then I took a black wig of

293

matted moss and Cuff's old straw hat which was in a most melancholy condition. Then I went waddling on stage, walking just like Cuff. You see, Cuff's walk always made people laugh so I thought it would be a good walk-on. Boy, the moment I got out on that stage that audience was quiet as a church. Before I got stage center I began to sing the verses I had been making up to that little 'jump Jim Crow' melody."

Daddy Rice could not resist singing:

> O, Jim Crow's come to town, as you all must know.
> An, he wheel about, he turn about, he do jiss so,
> An' ebery time he wheel about, he jump Jim Crow.

Emmett listened enchanted. Rice went on:

"The audience screamed with delight! I had made the impact of my career! Boy, the best was yet to come. That Cuff!" Daddy Rice went off into fits of laughter and Emmett waited. "Cuff was waiting in the wings frantic for his clothes. Now I forgot that a steamer was due any minute and for Cuff to be away from the wharf when a steamer came in would have blemished his reputation with the other bag carriers. Of course, it also meant that whatever tips he would get from this arrival would go to the others. Cuff reminded me of his existence. From stage left I could hear his desperate plea, 'Massa Rice . . . Massa Rice . . . must have my c'ose! Steamboat's comin'!' Of course, I couldn't pay any attention to Cuff at that moment.

"Suddenly I heard Cuff very distinctly call out, 'Massa Rice . . . Massa Rice . . . Steamboat's comin'! Must have them c'ose!'

"I could feel that he was frantic but I was busy with my own performance. The next time he repeated the words, the audience listened for them and laughed. Poor Cuff. He could wait no longer and driven by his desperation he rushed onto the stage in his tattered undress, this time shouting at me imperatively at the top of his voice, 'Massa Rice . . . Massa Rice . . . y' gimme mah niggah's hat . . . niggah's coat . . .

294

niggah's shoes! Now you gi' me mah niggah's t'ings! Steam-boat's comin'!'

"The audience screamed. Of course I had to go off with Cuff and give him his clothes fast, but that audience screamed for so long none of the other acts would go on and the curtain had to be lowered to empty the hall."

Rice put on a freshly laundered shirt, a vest, and slung his watch chain and fob across his middle. "Well," he reminisced as if a lifetime had passed, "that was just a few years ago. Now, boy, being blessed with only that same talent I have always had, I am a theatrical personage of some note."

Daddy Rice stood immaculately dressed for the street in the most magnificent suit Emmett had ever seen. The soldier was dazed by the vision before him. He had heard of Daddy Rice's eccentricities of dress before but what he saw defied belief. If he were not having hallucinations, the buttons on the great man's vest and coat were made of five- and ten-dollar gold pieces.

Rice watched the soldier with amusement. "Yes, you're seeing straight. Money—that's what money's for, boy, you *buy* decorations with it, or you just decorate with it." He yanked off a vest button. "Here you are, soldier boy," he said, handing Emmett the shiny coin. "Go buy yourself a treat!"

Dan Emmett remembered that day as if it were yesterday, his meeting with Daddy Rice. The memory of "Jump Jim Crow" lived with him not only through the rest of his army service until his discharge in 1835 but stayed with him as a model in the years that followed as he roamed the country first with one troupe and then with another.

Emmett could remember arriving in New York the autumn of 1842. He went immediately to his usual boardinghouse on Catherine Street in lower Manhattan. He was going to appear at the Bowery Theater for Bryant, the impresario. Staying at the same boardinghouse were three other black-face performers, all equally well known. There was Frank

295

Bower, a popular song-and-dance man, who at times did dramatic turns. There was Dick Pelham, whose real name was Richard Ward Bell and who had started out by appearing with Rice as Cuff, and there was Billy Whitlock, originally a typesetter on the *New York Herald,* who became a circus performer and had also taken the part of Cuff in Daddy Rice's play, *Oh, Hush.*

One evening early in February, 1843, the four were sprawling together in the sitting room of the boardinghouse. They were bored and debating whether or not a drink would be welcome. Emmett it was who pulled himself up from his armchair and declared, "We're all in a rut. Why don't we do something new and work together? Maybe create a new act like a minstrel troupe?"

Brower raised a sleepy eye, "Minstrel troupe? The audiences won't take it. They want a single minstrel who'll top the bill. They want to hear the words."

Billy Whitlock sat up suddenly. "He's got something! Leastways, he's right about one thing. Trouping's on its way out. We have to do something."

"I don't think trouping is on its way out," said Emmett, "but I think we need a change, so how about the four of us working up an act?"

Before the night was out, Emmett had his violin and banjo, Whitlock his banjo, Frank Brower the bones, and Pelham the tambourine. They were making music together. They inspired and amused each other. One would get up and do a turn, accompanied by the others. When he sat down, another got up. It was evident to them that they had something.

They practiced the act for a few days in Bartlett's billiard room. They worked tirelessly, rehearsing, improving, modifying, enlarging. They were exhilarated with their own ingenuity. They decided that their name should be the Virginia Minstrels.

It was on the night of February 6, 1843, that the following announcement appeared outside the Bowery Amphitheater:

296

"THE VIRGINIA MINSTRELS"

Being an exclusive Minstrel Entertainment

combining the Banjo, Violin,

Bone Castenets and the

Tambourine and entirely

exempt from the vulgarities

and other objectionable

features which have hitherto

characterized

Negro extravaganzas

When the curtain went up that night, the audience was the first privileged to see the Virginia Minstrels, wearing blackface and unique costumes designed by Emmett. This, destined to be the uniform of all minstrelmen, consisted of white trousers, striped calico shirt, and blue calico coat cut in exaggerated dress-suit style with a very elongated swallowtail. Each of the men took his turn being interlocutor and end man. Songs, skits, musical tidbits, jokes followed each other with endless rapidity. At the end of the performance the crowd was limp with laughter, and the Virginia Minstrels had made theatrical history.

For a year they played to packed houses in New York and Boston. Then in 1844 they followed the path of many head-liners of that day and this: they went to England. Oddly enough, while Daddy Rice and other single performers had taken England by storm, the Virginia Minstrels were a dismal flop. They were personally unhappy and the public did not receive them well. On their return to the United States they disbanded. However, all over the country other minstrel troupes had started in their absence. The country was minstrel crazy. Emmett's only comment on the London trip was: "The

297

only interesting thing that happened was the liberation of Daniel O'Connell, the Irish patriot, while I was in Dublin. What celebration! What a carrying on! It was a happy time in Dublin."

In America, Emmett found his personal popularity high. He toured the country, appearing as a headliner first with one company and then another. In 1853 he ventured to become an impresario by becoming part-owner of White's Minstrels in New York. He invested in the first minstrel hall in Chicago, in 1855, on Randolph Street.

In 1859 he was headlining with the Bryant brothers, Dan and Jerry, in New York. The Bryant brothers were to have a nine-year run with their troupe, Bryant's Minstrels, at Mechanic's Hall, which was between Grand and Broome Streets on Broadway. It was in the spring of that year, on a gloomy Saturday afternoon, that Jerry Bryant approached Emmett with a proposal. "Dan," he said, "we need a new song for the show. You're a music man. Why don't you write something for Monday's rehearsal?"

Dan looked up from lunch unenthusiastically, "You have not got me in a happy mood," he said. "I don't think I could write a song if my life depended on it."

"Well, the life of the show depends on it," Jerry Bryant said. "Our routines are beginning to drag. The audience knows what's coming next and if we don't do something to get them to sit up and take notice, we won't have any audience."

Emmett, stifling a yawn, mumbled, "Don't count on a masterpiece."

Immediately after lunch he picked up his violin and began to work out tunes, fragmentary bits of melody, old and new, which he hoped might inspire him or magically hold together in a cohesive song. Emmett struggled with this problem hour after hour, plodding ahead despite a nagging headache and the recurring thought that he had not the ability to add one and one together. This was Friday. By Sunday afternoon he was desperate. A fitful night's sleep had done nothing to refresh him, and the effort of holding the violin made it seem to weigh about two hundred pounds. The view outside his window did not help for it was a rainy, early spring day. Reflecting on his own inadequacy, Emmett muttered the current slang phrase used by all showmen who found themselves stranded up north in the wintertime: "I wish I was in Dixie land." He repeated the phrase, and it was the spark of inspiration out of the gloom. The violin came alive under his fingers, and within minutes he had worked out the pulsing rhythm of a new song.

At Monday's rehearsal, a smiling Dan Emmett showed up with a sheaf of music under his arm. Since he was usually dour, Jerry Bryant shouted, "Dan looks like the cat who swallowed the canary! What you got there, Dan?"

"Something so good even *your* troupe can play it."

The company gathered around him, clamoring to hear the new song. Emmett got up on a chair, gave himself an introduction on the violin and sang the first stanza:

> *Dis worl' was made in jiss six days,*
> *An' finish'd up in various ways,*
> *Look away! Look away! Look away! Dixie's Land!*
> *Dey den made Dixie trim an' nice,*
> *But Adam called it Paradise!*
> *Look away! Look away! Look away! Dixie's Land!*

By the time he finished singing the last verse, the whole company was marching around the rehearsal room, strutting, playing imaginary instruments, lustily joining in the chorus after hearing it only once. So excited was the company by the new number that Dan Emmett had to hold his violin high over his head to avoid getting it crushed in the back-slapping, bear-hugging, chest-pummeling to which he was subjected.

The song went into rehearsal immediately with only one change. Dan Bryant thought the first stanza might be misconstrued as sacrilegious. To avoid condemnation from any

299

quarter, the first verse was dropped, and the "Dixie" we know today was sung, beginning with the second original stanza: "I wish I was in de land ob cotton . . ."

The song immediately became popular. It spread from troupe to troupe and from city to city, and gradually the entire population of the country knew it. Then, two years later in New Orleans, the song began as a regional hymn, a battle refrain for the Confederacy . . . and a source of embarrassment to Dan Emmett.

At Appomattox, President Lincoln made the song "Dixie" a part of the Union again when he made this request: "I should like to hear the band play 'Dixie.' We have captured the Confederacy so now 'Dixie' belongs to us." Thus it was that Dan Emmett's sores were assuaged by peace.

For troupers, the old life re-established itself quickly. Jerry Bryant's Minstrels with Dan Emmett as headliner and lead man went off on tour immediately. When Bryant died in 1875, Dan Emmett, then sixty years old, became the leader of a permanent Chicago troupe, the Star Varieties.

It took Emmett another thirteen years to think of retiring but the winter of 1888 found him and his wife living quietly on a farm in Mount Vernon. So quiet was their life that his neighbors never associated him with *the* Dan Emmett, famous minstrel trouper.

It was in 1895 that a Columbus minstrel named Al G. Field arrived in Mount Vernon looking for Daniel Decatur Emmett. He stopped at one farmhouse and politely inquired, "Excuse me, ma'am, can you direct me to the home of Dan Emmett, the famous minstrelman?"

The farmer's wife could not help him. "No famous minstrelman living around here but there's a fellow named Emmett, a quiet old man living with his wife, a few miles down the road. Maybe it's some relative who can tell you where he is."

When Dan Emmett opened his farmhouse door, he let out

a whoop of delight. "Al! What are you doing out here in the middle of nowhere?"

"Looking for you, you scallywag," Field replied, embracing his friend. "Do you know I've been knocking on farmhouse doors looking for you for about a year. Well, aren't you going to ask me in?"

The atmosphere around the table that night was alive with reminiscence as the two minstrelmen swapped stories and anecdotes, and shared memories. "I'm not here just to find out about your health," Field announced. "I've come to ask you to make one more tour with me. Come out of retirement for just one more season——"

Dan interrupted him, "What can I do? I'm too old to hop around a stage like a grasshopper and my violin's been gathering dust for years."

"Do? All you gotta do is be there and come out after you are introduced as the man who wrote 'Dixie.' Then you sing a few bars. What you don't know is that 'Dixie' is the most famous song in the country and that you're an American institution. You gotta get off your rocking chair and come face the public. I tell you, they're dying to see you."

It was too much for Dan. He agreed to the tour. His first appearance was in Newark, Ohio, on August 22 of 1895. Of course he sang "Dixie," the catchy tune he had written thirty-six years before. In every city he was acclaimed, lauded, feted, medalled, congratulated, and adored. In Richmond, Virginia, he received the biggest ovation of his long stage career; for fully an hour the audience cheered and applauded, refusing to allow the old man off the stage.

"It was incredible," Emmett said later, somewhat shaken by the experience. "After all, I was a Union man during the war. Now I'm a hero because I accidentally gave them 'Dixie.'"

When the tour ended, Emmett refused the many lucrative offers which poured in. "This time I'm retiring for good," he said. He returned to Mount Vernon in the spring of 1896 to spend his final years in the peace and quiet of farm life with his wife. He died June 28, 1904.

A few months before his death, Emmett had agreed to be interviewed by a newspaperman, who asked him, "How much did you make out of writing 'Dixie,' Mr. Emmett?"

The old man paused, reflected, and replied, "Well, let's see, now. Five hundred dollars in cash . . . and a lifetime of satisfaction!"

To the Reader

I WAS BORN five years after Dan Emmett died, yet his songs are as real to me now as if I had heard them when they were first sung almost a hundred years ago. And so is his life—and so are the songs and lives of all those of whom I have written and sung. These are some of the people who make for me the picture of the America I love. It is of them I have written, and I hope that I have shared them well with you.

BURL IVES

BURL IVES was born June 14, 1909, in Jasper County in southern Illinois. His first professional performance took place when he was four years old at an Old Soldiers' Fourth of July picnic. Later he learned to play the banjo and at the age of twelve was a big success at a camp meeting in Hunt City, Illinois. He attended Illinois State Teachers College, but after two years the lure of music proved too strong and he picked up his guitar and took to the road.

In 1935, while studying German lieder in New York, he became more and more aware of the beauty and cultural importance of the folk music of the *English* language. From that time, he used every available means to make these songs and ballads known to the public. He has worked with schools and universities, made special recordings, given lectures and written articles for scholastic magazines. Steadily working with this material, he has, at the same time, maintained a full schedule as a performer in theater, radio, films, recordings, concerts, and television. In addition, he continues to add to his song collection and work creatively on his own repertoire. His autobiography, *Wayfaring Stranger*, and *The Burl Ives Song Book*, with its lucid notes on the history of our folk music, are well known.

With his wife and five-year-old son, Burl Ives lives alternately in a New York apartment and on a Bahaman ketch, the *Abaco Queen*.